pra___s for psychology

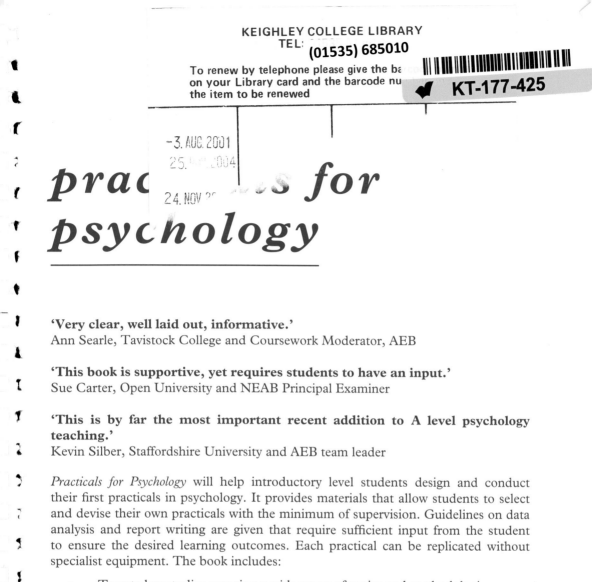

'**Very clear, well laid out, informative.**'
Ann Searle, Tavistock College and Coursework Moderator, AEB

'**This book is supportive, yet requires students to have an input.**'
Sue Carter, Open University and NEAB Principal Examiner

'**This is by far the most important recent addition to A level psychology teaching.**'
Kevin Silber, Staffordshire University and AEB team leader

Practicals for Psychology will help introductory level students design and conduct their first practicals in psychology. It provides materials that allow students to select and devise their own practicals with the minimum of supervision. Guidelines on data analysis and report writing are given that require sufficient input from the student to ensure the desired learning outcomes. Each practical can be replicated without specialist equipment. The book includes:

- Twenty key studies covering a wide range of topics and methodologies
- Points to think about, including the ethical and methodological issues raised by the studies
- A 'Do-it-yourself' section for each key study, showing students how to design their own practicals
- How to write up a practical, incorporating an actual student report with comments by an examiner
- Questionnaires and word lists

Practicals for Psychology is the ideal companion to coursework and practical work for students new to psychology. It will also be of interest to teachers and lecturers as resource material for discussing aspects of the whole research process.

Cara Flanagan is an experienced author and Assessor and Team Leader for AEB A level Psychology. Her previous publications include *Psychology A Level Study Guide* (1994), *Psychology GCSE Study Guide* (1995) and *Applying Psychology to Early Childhood Development* (1996). She is also co-editor of the *Routledge Modular Psychology* series (with Kevin Silber).

practicals for psychology

A STUDENT WORKBOOK

CARA FLANAGAN

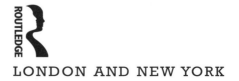

LONDON AND NEW YORK

First published 1998
by Routledge
11 New Fetter Lane, London EC4P 4EE

Simultaneously published in the USA and Canada
by Routledge
29 West 35th Street, New York, NY 10001

Typeset in Plantin and Rockwell by Keystroke,
Jacaranda Lodge, Wolverhampton
Printed and bound in Great Britain by
TJ International Ltd, Padstow, Cornwall

British Library Cataloguing in Publication Data
A catalogue record for this book is available from the British Library

Library of Congress Cataloging in Publication Data
A catalogue record for this book has been requested

ISBN 0–415–15774–9

*To Rob, Pip, Jack and Rosie,
with love*

CONTENTS

SOCIAL PSYCHOLOGY

OTHER

PREFACE

The impetus for writing this book came from being asked to provide material which would enable students to select and design their own practicals with minimal teacher supervision.

Some institutions have developed computer-based programs or handbooks to cope with the problem of having too many students and not enough time. Others give a large group of students a mini-lecture, followed by details of the method they are to follow, or outline some previous research and ask students to replicate it. I have chosen this latter approach because it gives the students an example to follow and build on. I see it as analogous to learning to cook – at the beginning you follow recipe books carefully, later you add your own ideas and innovations.

I have summarised a set of key studies to act as examples and also to give students a clear sense of the detailed way in which research is designed and reported, without consulting the original articles. The practicals included here can be used both as a starting point for individual research and/or as a basis for discussion about methodological and ethical issues. The book also provides students with models of how to organise a report.

The problem in writing a 'recipe book' for practicals is getting the balance right. Students need explicit information to help them plan their research and to outline good practice. At the same time there should be room for individual contribution and expression. I have tried to give students enough guidance to cope with their own project but have left plenty of room for individual input. There is no law that says you have to do what I say! I strongly advise *pilot studies* where time permits, and I also recommend that students start with simple projects – *don't be over ambitious*.

There are various questionnaires and word lists to help research design and a section on how to write the final report. I have not included a glossary because there are many good dictionaries which will supply this support. There is no section on research methodology and statistics for reasons of space, although there is an appendix giving brief guidance on statistics and a list of suitable reference books.

Some of the studies in this book are not new but have been included because they demonstrate more fundamental concepts and/or exemplify simpler research designs. More recent studies illustrate newer research techniques and changes in the approach to psychological research.

I would welcome any comments from teachers and students which would help improve the usefulness of this text. Meanwhile I hope it enhances your enjoyment of psychology and success in your course of study.

CARA FLANAGAN

HOW TO USE THIS BOOK

Each practical is organised on the basis of the following subheadings:

OUTLINE

A summary of the finding of the key study, details of what replication of the study would involve and a note about key issues related to the study.

INTRODUCTION

This is a brief introduction, much like the first part of a journal article, setting the scene for what is to follow. It is assumed that students will follow this up themselves using their own textbooks.

THE KEY STUDY

A summary of the research aims, questions and/or hypotheses.

METHOD

Details of participants, design, procedure and scoring, where relevant.

RESULTS

The tables, graphs and inferential tests used, and the reported significance of the key study – designed to inspire students on how to present (or not to present) their own results.

A note about analysis of variance (ANOVA) statistics: these have been included for the undergraduate reader and should not cause panic in anyone who doesn't think they have to know about them. Explanation is offered in Appendix II.

DISCUSSION

A conclusion and a few other noteworthy points.

ISSUES TO THINK ABOUT

A list of questions to help explore the pros and cons of the research design and results. A discussion of these should encourage students to design their own study better. There is a general list of questions at the end of this section, which can also be used.

REFERENCES

A list of articles cited in the text. Photocopies can be obtained through inter-library loans from any library for the cost of the photocopy.

RECOMMENDED READING

Some further articles to read.

OPTIMUM SEARCH STRATEGIES

Use the key words to find further information in the index of any textbook, from a CD-ROM such as PsycLit (available in most university libraries) or for searching the Internet.

DO-IT-YOURSELF: A SUGGESTED DESIGN

This is meant to be a starting point for your own research. Some students may want to follow it exactly, others may prefer to adapt it according to their own ideas.

GENERAL ISSUES AND QUESTIONS

After each practical there is an 'Issues to think about' section containing questions specific to that practical. Here is a general list of questions which you can answer and discuss in relation to each practical:

1   Write a suitable hypothesis for the study.
2   Name the independent and dependent variables (if an experimental design is being used).
3   What extraneous variables were there in the research?
4   What were the controls in the study?
5   What sampling technique was used?
6   What was the population from which the sample was drawn?
7   How would you briefly describe the kind of design that was followed?
8   What statistics (descriptive and inferential) were used or could be used?
9   Comment on the internal validity of the study.
10   To what extent could the study be described as 'ecologically valid'?
11   How could these results be applied to real life?
12   What ethical issues (if any) were dealt with by the researchers?
13   What other ethical issues were there?
14   For those interested in ANOVA statistics: Could you extend this study so that more than one independent variable was involved?

ACKNOWLEDGEMENTS

I would like to thank foremost Anthony Curtis for his encouragement and feedback, as well as Vivien Ward and Jon Reed at Routledge for easing me through the writing process with good humour and support. Kevin Silber has been a fount of information and advice as have Dennis Flanagan, Geraldine Flanagan and Rob Jones, for which I am ever grateful.

The author and publishers would like to thank all the copyright holders of material reproduced in this volume for granting permission to include it. Every effort has been made to contact authors and copyright holders, but without success in some cases. If proper acknowledgement has not been made, the copyright holder should contact the publishers.

practical
one

FRUIT MACHINE ADDICTION IN ADOLESCENCE

OUTLINE

This research takes a case study approach to exploring the problem of addiction to 'fruit machines', the 'one-arm bandits' that pay out when pictures of the same fruit appear. The study chronicles one teenage boy's descent into pathological gambling behaviour and his subsequent recovery. The insights afforded support previous research as well as suggesting ideas for future investigations. Replication would call for examining more 'normal' behaviour because of ethical concerns. A key issue is the value of qualitative research.

INTRODUCTION

Addiction refers to an individual's dependence on a substance or activity. Many drugs create a *physiological* dependence as well as a *psychological* one. Physiological dependence is characterised by the development of tolerance and the difficulty of withdrawal. Tolerance refers to the fact that the body increasingly adapts to the substance and needs larger doses to achieve the same effect. Withdrawal results in craving, anxiety, hallucinations and other physical symptoms.

Psychological withdrawal may have similar effects. Moreover, it is characterised as being self-reinforcing – the pleasurable effects of a substance or activity increase the likelihood of continuing with it as do the negative effects of withdrawal. Addicts also often develop a social life centred around the addiction, which increases the difficulty in stopping.

Addiction is included in the DSM-IV (*Diagnostic and Statistical Manual of Mental Disorders*, 4th edition, 1994, of the American Psychiatric Association) classification of abnormal behaviour. There is one section for substance-related disorders and another on impulse-control disorders which includes pathological gambling. Fruit machines are potentially addictive because of the high or rapid staking associated with them (Griffiths, 1997). Other reasons for the addiction include easy availability, instant reward and a mistaken sense of subjective probability – people tend to overestimate their chance of success and underestimate their chance of failure.

Research suggests that 65% of adolescents gamble at some point, and 10% to 20% do so at least once a week. For a small number (between 1% and 6%) their gambling might be regarded as pathological, as defined in the DSM (Griffiths, 1993a).

the key study

Griffiths (1993a) noted that most studies on fruit machine gambling in adolescence have concentrated on the incidence and demographics of the gamblers, and have conducted quantitative analyses of their motivations, subjective feelings and so on (for example, Lesieur and Klein, 1987). Griffiths felt that greater understanding of the problem might be gained from an in-depth study of one individual.

METHOD

Participants

'David' aged 18, and his mother. The mother got in touch with Mark Griffiths as a result of a postal survey which he had conducted on gambling behaviour (Griffiths, 1993b).

Design/Procedure

Most of the data were collected in separate interviews with the mother and her son, though some were collected in correspondence. The data consisted of mainly retrospective recollections.

Since the study was based on personal reports, the 'results section [was] far from academic in the traditional sense'.

RESULTS

David had one younger sister and grew up in a seaside town. Up to the age of 14, in his mother's words, he was 'a lovely, lively boy, clever at school and good at sports . . . someone I could be proud of'. During the next four years he became 'a miserable, withdrawn and rebellious son'.

The beginning of the problem

David's swimming club and his school reported to his parents that he was often late and didn't appear to be interested in anything. At that stage his parents put his problems down to 'adolescence', although they noticed that he went out most evenings. His mother pleaded with him not to go out so much, but 'it didn't seem to make any difference. He would just go. He seemed to have completely lost respect for us'. They thought he might be involved with drugs, but once when his mother followed him discreetly, she saw that he went into an amusement arcade. It seemed he was just occupied with 'harmless fun'.

Then his mother and sister realised that money was going missing. David denied that he had anything to do with it. At this point his family began to suspect he had a gambling problem.

David's story

David first used fruit machines on family holidays. There were also machines where he went swimming and at his workplace, a restaurant.

He realised he had become compulsive but didn't think there was anything serious about it. He only worried where he was going to get money and didn't feel concerned about who he might hurt in the process. He earned £60 a week in the restaurant but spent it immediately. There was one period when he managed to save £100 towards the cost of a motorbike.

This was followed, however, by a series of family rows, and he returned to gambling full-time. He sold the motorbike and spent the £400 proceeds in one day.

Family distress

The more rows David had with his parents, the more he shut himself away, psychologically and physically, and continued gambling – which led to more rows. It was a vicious circle. His parents wondered whether the best thing would be to give him money to stop the stealing, or whether it would be better to just turn him out of the house.

Why did David continue?

'I always got the feeling of being "high" or "stoned". . . . Although winning money was the first thing that attracted me to playing fruit machines, this gradually converted to light, sounds and excitement.'

'I couldn't even spend time to worry about the amounts of money I was pouring in, in fact it's hard to think what was actually going through my mind. All I can remember is a total blank.' He was 'living in a trance for nearly four years'.

'I was always very upset about losing all my money and I returned many times to try to win back my losses . . . [though] I never believed that I would win it back. . . . The only time I found it possible to think about giving up was after leaving the arcade at closing time and [vowing] never to return.'

'Whenever I felt depressed (which was practically all the time) or rejected, the urge to play machines became even bigger. Whenever I had to make a slight effort in my life, I needed to counteract it by gambling.' For example, at one time David did a paper round every morning but then had to go to the arcade immediately afterwards to cope with the stress created by the job.

At first David enjoyed showing off his skills to his friends, but in time he started to gamble alone, and then his skills only mattered as a means of stretching out the money he had to gamble with.

His mother described his addiction: 'He couldn't wait for the doors of the arcade to open in the mornings. He hammered on them in frustration. . . . He was unable to concentrate on anything except his need to be there.' His personality changed – he became evasive, withdrawn and argumentative. His appearance changed too – he didn't wash and went to school in smelly clothes.

Recovery

When David's mother was able to finally admit to herself how much David had been spending and the seriousness of the problem, she confronted him and he told her everything. 'That was the first massive step towards reaching the light at the end of the tunnel.'

David's mother got in touch with Gamblers Anonymous and David said, 'It was marvellous . . . there are people there who I can talk to who know exactly how I feel.' This meant that David was able to accept that he had a problem. 'I was able to talk . . . instead of playing the machines and [it] enabled me to GIVE UP. There was no method, just sheer will-power and the fact that I wanted to give up.' He also practised yoga, to relax when he felt the pull to gamble again, and he stayed well away from fruit machines.

His mother realises that he is not cured: 'a life crisis might trigger the need to go back to his addiction.' David is quite positive, although he feels bad about the harm he did to others and his lost education. 'I will have to live with these mental scars for the rest of my life.'

Summary

The behaviour patterns recorded here displayed all the classic features of addiction:

- Salience: All day was spent thinking about gambling or doing it.
- Tolerance: Increasingly more time and money was spent on gambling.
- Chasing: David kept returning to win back losses.
- Euphoria and dysphoria: Getting high and then feeling depressed.
- Withdrawal: Anguish felt on being deprived of gambling.
- Relapse: Returning full-time to gambling after periods of stopping.

David's recovery also resulted from classic techniques to overcome addiction:

- Talking with his mother.
- Sharing feelings with other addicts, and getting their support.
- Relaxation to deal with stress rather than relapsing.
- Behavioural self-monitoring: staying away from the machines.
- Personal motivation.

DISCUSSION

It is hazardous to generalise from a case study, but the data collected do highlight important issues, which may be overlooked in quantitative analyses.

Typically, the development and maintenance of gambling behaviour can be explained by sociological and psychological factors. In this case study an important sociological factor was the easy access to gambling machines. As for psychological factors, initial motivations included winning money, displaying skill and having fun. Motivation to continue was almost entirely escapist, created by feelings of depression, confusion and rejection. What had been a primary motivator – money – became a means to an end. Biological factors could include the possibility of a 'pleasure centre' in the brain (Olds and Milner, 1954).

One of the key themes in the study was the lack of family communication and support. David felt that he had no one to turn to and that gambling was a way of coping with family tensions. When his mother finally did confront him he began to deal with the problem. Just one meeting with Gamblers Anonymous changed his perspective, which might explain why such self-help groups have large drop-out rates. The study also indicates the importance of relaxation techniques as a means of resisting relapse.

Qualitative research is important in identifying areas for further research. For example, in this study the role of depression has been identified as an antecedent of gambling. Such research can also offer useful insights that might help therapists to relate better to their clients.

ISSUES TO THINK ABOUT

1 What is/are the research aims of this study?
2 Distinguish between qualitative and quantitative research.
3 In reading this summary of a case study, what do you feel are the particular benefits of its approach?
4 Reliance on quotations is called 'giving voice'. To what extent do you think this is truly representative of what the person actually thinks? Is 'giving voice' subject to researcher bias?
5 Many of the data in this study were retrospective. How do you feel this may have affected the results?
6 In a study such as this, how might one control for the unreliability of retrospective data?
7 What did Griffiths mean when he said that the 'results section is far from academic in the traditional sense'?
8 Describe one or more insights this study has given you into pathological gambling.
9 To what extent do you think a study such as this one affords

> greater understanding of gambling addiction than a survey-type study?
>
> 10 This study had an 'ending'. In what way would the approach be different if one were studying a continuing addiction?

REFERENCES

Griffiths, M.D. (1993a) Fruit machine addiction in adolescence: A case study. *Journal of Gambling Studies, 9(4)*, 387–99.

Griffiths, M.D. (1993b) Factors in problem adolescent fruit machine gambling: Results of a small postal survey. *Journal of Gambling Studies, 9*, 31–45.

Griffiths, M.D. (1997) Selling hope: The psychology of the National Lottery. *Psychology Review, 4(1)*, 26–30.

Lesieur, H.R. and Klein, R. (1987) Pathological gambling among high school students. *Addictive Behaviours, 12*, 129–35.

Olds, J. and Milner, P. (1954) Positive reinforcement produced by electrical stimulation of the septal area and other regions of the rat brain. *Journal of Comparative and Physiological Psychology, 47*, 419–28.

RECOMMENDED READING

Fisher, S. (1993) The pull of the fruit machine: A sociological typology of young players. *Sociological Review, 41*, 444–72.

Griffiths, M.D. (1990) The acquisition, development and maintenance of fruit machine gambling in adolescence. *Journal of Gambling Studies, 6*, 193–204.

OPTIMUM SEARCH STRATEGIES

Key terms: Pathological gambling, addiction, dependence, fruit machines, adolescence, depression, family conflict.

Do-it-yourself: A Suggested Design

Research aim and questions   To investigate an ethically 'safe' area of human behaviour with the case study approach, for example, the experience of taking examinations.

- Do exam candidates suffer from minor and major physical symptoms before and after taking exams?
- Do exam candidates feel most stressed when they are tired?
- What study strategies lead exam candidates to feel they have worked most effectively?

Participants   One person before and after taking exams.

Design   This is a case study.

- Interview the main 'case' together with associated individuals such as teachers, parents and friends. It is important to be a good questioner and to be adaptable. Practice (a pilot study) will help you to develop questions/methods to elicit further information.
- Develop further research questions as you go along.
- Interviews should be continuing, at intervals decided by you, so that an in-depth picture is built up. You might also ask individuals to keep their own diaries and answer specific questions.
- Record any relevant facts, such as previous exam results, school attitudes and health records. Record any events during the period of your study, such as illness and amount of time spent revising.
- Psychometric tests or attitude scales can be employed, depending on issues of confidentiality and your experience as a tester. You might use a simple means of assessing stress by asking the 'case' to rate his/her stress level daily on a scale of 1 to 10.

Ethical considerations
- You should remember informed consent, avoid any deception or causing unnecessary distress and respect confidentiality and privacy.
- You should record data anonymously and debrief all participants, offering them the right to withhold their data.

Controls
- Careful and unbiased questioning. Avoid too many yes/no questions. Avoid talking too much. Avoid leading questions.

Materials
- Tape recorder.

Analysis
- Giving voice: use quotes to represent your findings, alongside descriptions of behaviour.
- Thematic analysis: organise your results in terms of the themes you initially identified or those that have emerged.
- Descriptive statistics: for example, represent stress data over time with means, clearly labelled tables and graphs.
- Related test of difference: compare participant's stress levels before and after exams.

practical two

LATERAL DOMINANCE AND AESTHETIC PREFERENCE

OUTLINE

This study compares right- and left-handers in terms of their preferences for right and left visual fields, finding a significant difference. This illustrates one aspect of brain lateralisation and raises questions about the evolution of language. Replication calls for the preparation of a set of slides or overhead transparencies. Each picture is shown twice to a group of participants, once 'normal' and once reversed. A key issue is the technique used to obtain participants (sampling).

INTRODUCTION

Lateralisation refers to the fact that the brain is divided into two sides or halves (hemispheres). Some functions are represented in both halves, whereas other functions, such as language, are usually found on one side only (the right or the left). For some functions, such as memory, both sides of the brain function equally. For other functions one side is dominant. This is true of motor processes; most people have a preferred 'side' for writing or kicking a ball. Motor processes are also contralateral – one hemisphere controls the opposite side of the body, so that if a person is right-handed it is their left hemisphere that is dominant.

It has also been found that most right-handed people have a visual preference for the left visual field, probably because the right hemisphere is dominant for visuo-spatial tasks. This has been demonstrated by Levy *et al.* (1972) who studied 'split-brain' patients (patients whose left and right hemispheres had been separated by injury or brain surgery). Levy *et al.* found that when the two visual fields of the patients were shown different pictures, the patients usually selected the pictures seen by the right hemisphere. In another study Nelson and McDonald (1971) found that when participants were asked to select titles for a picture, they were most likely to select titles that corresponded to the content on the left-hand side. They explained this in terms of right-side aesthetic dominance.

the key study

Levy (1976) investigated this attentional bias, suggesting that if the direction of hemispheric specialisation does affect preferences for left and right visual fields, we would expect left- and right-handers to display different response patterns. This follows from evidence (Levy, 1974) that 99% of right-handers have left hemisphere language organisation and 44% of left-handers have a reversed pattern of organisation.

The hypothesis therefore was that left- and right-handers display different response patterns for aesthetic preference.

METHOD

Participants

Of 145 introductory psychology students, all 'American-born native readers of English', 31 were left-handers as determined by self-report. Those who described themselves as 'ambidextrous' were included in the left-hander group. There were 61 females and 84 males.

Design

Ninety-seven vacation photograph slides were the stimulus. They were shown to the participants in pairs of identical slides, with one slide reversed.

Procedure

Each slide was exposed for 15 seconds, and then participants were given a further 15 seconds to choose the member of each pair they preferred.

Scoring procedure

1. In order to determine a modal response for the right-handers, Levy randomly chose 31 right-handed males and found 14 slides for which there was considerable agreement about which version was preferable. This was used to establish a 'preferred' and 'non-preferred' standard.

2. For all remaining participants (N=114) a score between +100 and –100 was calculated in the following way. A participant who chose all the preferred versions of the target 14 slides would get +100 and a participant who chose all the non-preferred versions would get –100. A participant who selected seven preferred versions would score zero. Intermediate scores were calculated on a pro-rata basis; for example, selecting 10 preferred slides would provide a ratio of 3:7 equivalent to 42.86 out of 100, a score of 43.

Any bias produced by this method would result in an underestimate of the difference between right- and left-handers.

RESULTS

The mean score of right-handers significantly differed from zero in a positive direction, whereas this was not true for the score of left-handers (see Table 2.1). The scores of right- and left-handers also significantly differed from each other.

Table 2.1 Preference scores for 114 right- and left-handers

Comparison	df	Mean	t
Right-handers versus zero	82	22.69	7.61**
Left-handers versus zero	30	6.89	1.22
Right- versus left-handers	112	15.70	2.65**

** = $p < .005$, one-tailed.
Source: Reprinted from Levy (1976) with permission from Elsevier Science.

DISCUSSION

This study provides strong support for the role of cerebral lateralisation in determining aesthetic preference but does not suggest why it might be so. Asymmetry would be a disadvantage in terms of motor responses, because an organism would respond in a biased way. Therefore there must be some fitness advantage that could explain how lateralisation evolved. One possibility is the appearance of language in higher animals. Mixed dominance would create competing language centres, and mixed dominance has been found to be associated with problems such as stuttering and dyslexia (see, e.g., Jones, 1966).

A subsequent study by Levy and Kueck (1986) confirmed earlier evidence that pictures with greater content on the right were the ones more strongly preferred by right-handers.

ISSUES TO THINK ABOUT

1 Levy describes his participants as 'American-born native readers of English'. Why might this be significant in this particular study?
2 Levy decided to include ambidextrous individuals in the left-hander group. Do you think this could be a source of bias? What would you have done with ambidextrous individuals?
3 Do you think there might be problems collecting a representative sample for a study such as this one? Why?
4 Handedness was determined by self-report. Do you think this was a valid means of assessment?
5 Do you feel the method used to assess which slide each participant preferred was a valid measure?
6 It is suggested that any bias produced by this method would result in an underestimate of the difference between right- and left-handers. Why is this desirable?
7 In the original article, Levy suggested that 'undoubted Type I errors contributed to [the] scores' of the 31 right-handed males whose preferences were used to set the standard. What is meant by a Type 1 error in this context?
8 Do you think that the subject matter or content of the slides could make a significant difference to the results? How? Would other material (such as faces) be better than using vacation photographs? Why?
9 Explain how the degrees of freedom were calculated in Table 2.1.
10 Why might this be called a quasi-experiment?

REFERENCES

Jones, R.K. (1966) Observations on stammering after localised cerebral injury. *Journal of Neurology, Neurosurgery, and Psychiatry*, *29*, 192–5.

Levy, J. (1974) Psychobiological implications of bilateral assymmetry. In S. Diamond and J.G. Beamont (eds) *Hemisphere function in the human brain*. London: Paul Elek.

Levy, J. (1976) Lateral dominance and aesthetic preference. *Neuropsychologia*, *14*, 431–45.

Levy , J. and Kueck, L. (1986) A right hemispatial field advantage on a verbal free-vision task. *Brain and Language*, *27*, 24–37.

Levy, J., Trevarthen, C. and Sperry, R. (1972) Perception of bilateral chimeric figures following hemispheric deconnexion. *Brain*, *95*, 61–78.

Nelson, T. and Macdonald, G. (1971) Lateral organisation, perceived depth and title preference in pictures. *Perceptual and Motor Skills*, *33*, 983–6.

RECOMMENDED READING

Kinsbourne, M. and McMurray, J. (1975) The effect of cerebral dominance on time sharing between speaking and tapping by preschool children. *Child Development*, *46*, 240–2.

Rosenfield, D.B. and Goodglass, H. (1980) Dichotic testing of cerebral dominance in stutterers. *Brain and Language*, *11*, 170–80.

OPTIMUM SEARCH STRATEGIES

Key terms: Lateralisation, aesthetic preference, handedness, left-handers (sinister versus dextral), visual field, hemispatial.

Do-it-yourself: A Suggested Design

Hypothesis   Left- and right-handers display different response patterns for aesthetic preference.

Participants   Anyone.

Design   This is an independent measures quasi-experiment.

- Prepare a set of slides or overhead transparencies. You will need two copies of each slide or overhead transparency so that one can be shown reversed. The pictures should be novel to prevent any participants from having preconceived preferences.
- Decide how to determine handedness. You could observe the participants writing their names or you could ask them to state their preferred handedness.

Ethical considerations

- Since this experiment involves deception, you should take special care with debriefing, providing *post-hoc* informed consent.
- You should avoid causing any unnecessary distress, respect confidentiality and offer participants the right to withhold their data.

Controls

- Single blind.
- Careful sampling to ensure a reasonable spread of left-handers.
- Standardised instructions and conditions.

Materials

- Slides or overhead transparencies that are unfamiliar to the participants.
- Response sheets.
- Standardised instructions and debriefing notes.

Analysis

- Descriptive statistics: means, clearly labelled tables and graphs.
- Randomly select a group of right-handed participants. Select a set of pictures about which there is close agreement in terms of preference. Call this view the preferred view (P). The reverse is the non-preferred view (NP).
- Score all participants using this designation. In this way you can say whether the preferences of one group of right-handers was predictive of all right-handers, and whether it was the same or different from the left-handers.
- Unrelated test of difference: to compare the two groups.

practical three

FOOTBALL KNOWLEDGE AND MEMORY

OUTLINE

This study demonstrates how memory is enhanced by prior knowledge or the existence of schemas. People who know a lot about football are better able to recall football scores than people who don't. Their schemas facilitate encoding and recall. To replicate this study you need to construct a questionnaire and test participants' recall of a set of football results. One group of participants can be tested together. A key issue is conducting research in a real-world setting.

INTRODUCTION

Memory research focused for many years on artificial tasks such as learning lists of CVCs (consonant–vowel–consonant) and subsequently recalling them. In the past few decades interest has shifted to memory tasks that are more characteristic of real life. The distinction made between different kinds of memory has helped. Cohen and Squire (1980) divided long-term memory into a procedural system (knowing how to do things) and a declarative system (knowledge about facts). Tulving (1972) suggested that the declarative system could be subdivided into episodic memory (knowledge about personal events and people) and semantic memory (linguistic and general knowledge). It tends to be episodic memory that is tested in laboratory memory experiments.

Examples of real-world memory research include a study by Ley (1978), which focused on how doctors might improve their patients' recall of medical instructions. Another area which has received attention is memory for the positions of chess pieces (Chase and Simon, 1973). Expert players are better at recalling the position of pieces as long as they have been placed in a configuration resembling a real game. If the pieces are randomly placed, there is no difference in performance between experts and non-experts. It is suggested that this happens because experts group known configurations into higher-order units that facilitate memory.

the key study

Morris et al. *(1981) observed that many football enthusiasts are able to remember match scores after having heard a set of results only once. This recall is equivalent to a laboratory paired-associate task – people are given a list of artificially paired items (words, nonsense syllables or digits) and then given one member of the pair and asked to recall the other. In a laboratory, if a participant was asked to recall a list of 120 words paired randomly with a digit (such as Manchester–1) performance would be very poor. Let alone two words and two digits (such as Leeds–2 Leicester–0).*

The research questions were:

- *'Do experts in and enthusiasts for a particular subject acquire new information about their special interest more easily than novices?'*
- *'If so, what processes explain this more rapid acquisition?'*

METHOD

Participants

Thirty-eight male undergraduates who had been paid 50p each.

Design

Football knowledge was assessed with a questionnaire. The questions included some very simple ones, so that it was possible to distinguish those participants who knew a little about football from those who knew nothing. There were 42 questions in all, covering a range of competitions, for example:

- Who is Manchester City's goalkeeper?
- Who plays at Brisbane Road?
- Who were the last English team to win the EUFA cup?
- Who is the manager of Celtic?

Procedure

The participants were tested in a group on a Saturday afternoon. First, they were given the questionnaire. They then listened to the live football results (64 matches) and finally they were asked to write down as many of the results as they could remember on a sheet listing the fixtures. They had been asked not to listen to any football reports on the afternoon before the experiment.

Recall of football scores was marked correct only if both scores were remembered correctly.

Control

It is possible that the football enthusiasts guessed the scores more accurately than those participants who knew little or nothing about football. This hypothesis was tested by asking another group of participants (24 male undergraduates) to predict the scores in advance of the matches being played. Their successes were correlated with the scores in the football knowledge questionnaire.

RESULTS

The questionnaire scores were bimodally distributed: 16 participants had fewer than 5 correct, 16 scored between 20 and 30 and 4 scored about 30.

Spearman's rank order correlations were calculated because of this bimodal distribution. Those participants with greater football knowledge had a better recall of scores (see Table 3.1). This was particularly true for First Division (now Premier League) results, about which participants presumably had greater knowledge.

There was no significant correlation between the control group's football knowledge and their ability to predict correct results.

Table 3.1 Scores recalled or predicted and the correlations between recall or prediction and performance on the football knowledge questionnaire

| | | | | | | Divisions | | |
| | | English | | | | | Scottish | |
	Overall	First	Second	Third	Fourth	Premier	First	Second
Experimental group:								
Mean scores recalled	14.9	5.6	2.5	2.1	2.1	0.8	0.3	1.5
Correlation ($N=38$)	0.81**	0.79**	0.71**	0.39*	0.47**	0.31**	0.34**	0.19
Control group:								
Mean scores predicted correctly	4.3	0.8	0.6	1.1	0.7	0.4	0.4	0.3
Correlation ($N=24$)	0.3	0.27	−0.11	0.09	0.18	0.11	0.12	0.10

$* = p<.05$ $** = p<.01$

Source: Reprinted with permission from Morris *et al.* (1981). Copyright © The British Psychological Society.

DISCUSSION

Clearly football knowledge is associated with better recall of football results. Such performance cannot be due to informed guessing, because the control group did not produce significant results. The football 'expert' encodes the results more effectively than others, and this was especially true for First Division results.

It could be that individuals who could recall information for the questionnaire have better memories and therefore did well when they were recalling the scores. This is considered unlikely because intercorrelations of performance on different memory tasks are usually low.

Morris *et al.* (1981) reject the concept of greater 'interest' as being too vague to be a helpful explanation of why football experts do better. In any case all the participants must have been motivated to learn because they knew they would be tested. Instead, Morris *et al.* suggest, it is because experts' richer knowledge is activated when they hear the results. They want to fit this new information into existing schemas such as what the consequences of the results might be for league positions. However, richer encoding doesn't necessarily lead to better recall. It may be that the names of football clubs act as better retrieval cues for the experts.

There are therefore two processes at work. Encoding is enhanced by prior knowledge because it aids elaboration. Recall is improved because retrieval cues have greater meaning for those with more knowledge.

ISSUES TO THINK ABOUT

1   Was it necessary to pay the participants? How might payment or nonpayment affect the participants' performance?
2   Why was it necessary to include some easy questions in the questionnaire? What might have happened if the questions were all very hard? Were the experimenters trying to avoid a floor or ceiling effect?
3   Why was it necessary to cover a range of different competitions?
4   Why did the study use live football results?
5   Morris *et al.* chose to accept as correct only those answers that had both scores right. Could they have used an alternative scoring system? Which is preferable?
6   Spearman's rank order correlation was used. Why was this choice necessary and what was the alternative?
7   Were there other factors you feel should have been controlled in the study?
8   Was it necessary to test recall of *all* the results?

9   Morris *et al.* suggested that those participants who did better on the questionnaire have better memories and therefore did well when recalling the scores. Do you think this could explain the results of the study?

10   What kind of memory was tested in the study?

11   Is this study gender biased?

REFERENCES

Chase, W.G. and Simon, H.A. (1973) Perception in chess. *Cognitive Psychology, 4,* 55–81.

Cohen, N.J. and Squire, L.R. (1980) Preserved learning and retention of pattern-analysing skill in amnesia using perceptual learning. *Cortex, 17,* 273–8.

Ley, P. (1978) Memory for medical information. In M.M. Gruneberg, P.E. Morris and R.N. Sykes (eds) *Practical aspects of memory.* London: Academic Press.

Morris, P.E., Gruneberg, M.M., Sykes, R.N. and Merrick, A. (1981) Football knowledge and the acquisition of new results. *British Journal of Psychology, 72,* 479–83.

Tulving, E. (1972) Episodic and semantic memory. In E. Tulving and W. Donaldson (eds) *Organisation of memory.* London: Academic Press.

RECOMMENDED READING

Cohen, C.E. (1981) Person categories and social perception: Testing some boundaries of the processing effects of prior knowledge. *Journal of Personality and Social Psychology, 40,* 441–52.

OPTIMUM SEARCH STRATEGIES

Key terms: Real-world memory, football, schemas, episodic memory, semantic memory, procedural memory, declarative memory, recall, paired-associate.

Do-it-yourself: A Suggested Design

Hypothesis   Recall of football results is positively correlated with performance on a football questionnaire.

Participants   Anyone, to include people having a range of football knowledge.

Design   This is a correlational study using a questionnaire.

- Compile a football questionnaire to assess football knowledge. The questions should vary in difficulty to ensure a good spread of scores. You might do a pilot study of the questionnaire.
- Arrange to test a group of participants when the football results are being broadcast, or invent your own results (though this will be much less effective).
- Write standardised instructions and prepare a recall sheet, with fixture names on it.

Ethical considerations
- Since this experiment involves deception, you should take special care with debriefing, providing *post-hoc* informed consent.
- You should avoid causing any unnecessary distress, respect confidentiality and offer participants the right to withhold their data.

Controls
- Varied questions to provide a good spread of scores.
- Single blind.
- Standardised instructions and conditions.

Materials
- Football knowledge questionnaire.
- Football results.
- Standardised instructions and debriefing notes.

Analysis
- Descriptive statistics: means, clearly labelled tables and graphs.
- Test of correlation: use Spearman's rank order test if the results are not normally distributed otherwise you can use Pearson's test.
- Alternative: divide your participants into experts and non-experts and use an unrelated test of difference to compare recall performances. Take care when choosing your criteria for grouping.

practical four

EYEWITNESS IDENTIFICATION

OUTLINE

This experiment demonstrates that when people are unlikely to remember accurate details they rely on surprisingly obvious clues. The study simulates the behaviour of eyewitnesses identifying suspects in a police line-up. Replication calls for use of a set of photographs. Key issues are the ethics of field experiments and ecological validity.

INTRODUCTION

Brown (1986) wrote that the paradox of eyewitness identification is that professionals (psychologists, solicitors, judges) regard it as the least trustworthy kind of evidence, whereas jurors find it more persuasive than any other kind. There is a frightening history of criminal cases where witnesses have identified the wrong person (in some cases as many as 30 witnesses), and cases where a jury has chosen to believe eyewitness testimony in spite of much evidence to the contrary.

One remedy is for a defence attorney to call an expert witness in order to convince a jury that the eyewitness testimony may well be unreliable. Elizabeth Loftus (1979) was asked to do just that in the trial of José Garcia, who was accused of murdering a shop assistant during a robbery. The only evidence of Garcia's guilt was the testimony of a witness – a second shop assistant, Joseph Melville. Loftus argued, for example, that the fact that Garcia was identified by Melville two weeks after the crime meant that the identification may well have been mistaken because memory trace decays over time. It was also true that Melville had been in a state of extreme distress after seeing his colleague shot, and research has shown that people remember things less reliably when they are under high levels of stress. Race is another important factor – Garcia was a Mexican-American and Melville was white; research has shown that people are less able to identify members of another ethnic group than they are members of their own.

Both perception and memory function effectively by being selective and constructive. They both rely heavily on top-down processes to 'fill in the gaps' and are thus affected by prejudices and by leading questions or clues. Loftus *et al.*'s classic study (1978) demonstrated that leading questions affected the responses of experimental participants. The use of 'a' or 'the' in a question changed the way a person answered the question. 'Did you see the broken headlight?' assumes that there was a headlight, whereas 'Did you see a broken headlight?' is more open-ended.

Incidentally, in the Garcia trial, the jury could not agree on a verdict and Garcia was acquitted.

the key study

Buckhout (1974) suggested that 'research and courtroom experience provide ample evidence that an eyewitness to a crime is asked to do something and be something that a normal human being was not created to be or do'. Buckhout identified various key features of the crime scene that make subsequent recall likely to be inaccurate, such as the fact that what is seen often has no significance at the time; that the scene is usually viewed under less than ideal conditions and in a state of distress; that perception is likely to rely on perceptual set which inevitably introduces systematic biases; and that witnesses may unconsciously conform with other witnesses. Later on, identification may be biased by leading questions and unfair line-up tests.

Buckhout tested this last hypothesis in his own study – how does the way suspects are presented bias the identification process?

METHOD

Participants

One hundred and forty-one 'witnesses' and a second group of 52 participants who had not seen the original incident.

Design

An assault was staged on a university campus: a student attacked a professor while one bystander and the witnesses watched. The incident was videotaped in order to compare true events with eyewitness reports.

Subsequent identification was tested with a set of six photographs that included both the attacker and the 'innocent bystander'. There were four experimental conditions:

- Unbiased picture spread (see Figure 4.1): the portraits were aligned and all were similar full-face views.
- Biased picture spread (see Figure 4.2): the attacker's head was tilted, he was grinning and the photograph was placed at an angle.
- Low-bias instructions: witnesses were asked if they recognised anybody.
- High-bias instructions: witnesses were reminded of the incident and told, 'one of these men is a suspect in the assault we saw. It is important that you identify him for us.'

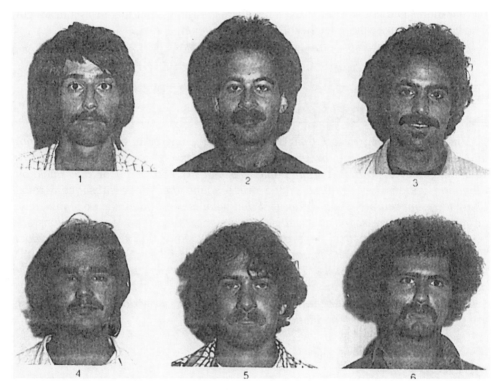

Figure 4.1 Unbiased picture spread shown to some participants. The portraits were aligned and showed similar full-face views
Source: Buckhout (1974)

Procedure

After the attack a sworn statement was taken from each of the witnesses, asking them to describe the suspect, the clothes he was wearing and whatever else they could remember. They were also asked to rate their own confidence in the accuracy of their description.

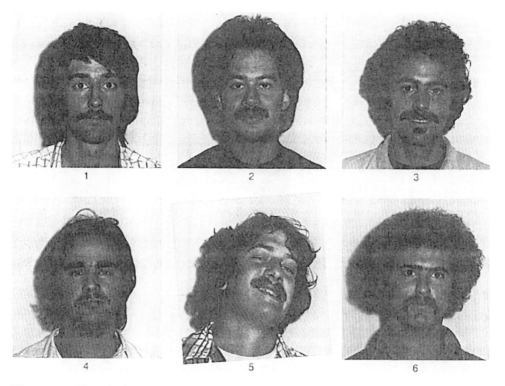

Figure 4.2 Biased picture spread. The attacker's photograph was tilted and his expression was different
Source: Buckhout (1974)

Seven weeks later witnesses were asked to identify the attacker from one of the layouts shown in Figures 4.1 and 4.2.

The second group of participants didn't see the original incident but had it described to them. They were shown the photographs under the same experimental conditions and were asked to identify the most likely perpetrator.

RESULTS

Only 40% of the witnesses identified the suspect correctly; 25% identified the innocent bystander instead. Even the professor selected the wrong person.

Participants who were given the biased picture spread and the high-bias instructions gave the highest proportion of correct responses at 61%, and participants in this condition were also the most confident in their choice (see Figure 4.3).

When the participants who had not seen the original incident were shown the picture spread, they too were most likely to pick out Number 5.

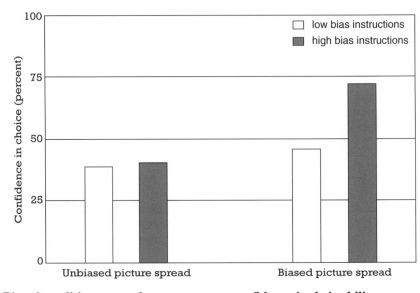

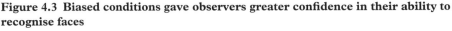

Figure 4.3 Biased conditions gave observers greater confidence in their ability to recognise faces
Source: Buckhout (1974)

DISCUSSION

The evidence presented here suggests that witnesses can be easily swayed in the identifications they make. One might think that they would *avoid* the obvious choice, but this is not so, supporting the view that when people are uncertain, they rely on any clues available. The experiment has ecological validity because in many eyewitness situations, the people involved may well be uncertain and be put under pressure to make an identification.

In a later study Buckhout (1980) arranged for a film of a purse being snatched to be shown on the television news. This was followed by a line-up of six men and viewers were invited to ring in – 2,145 did so but only 14% were correct. This is actually slightly worse than a random level of guessing (1/6 = 16.7%).

ISSUES TO THINK ABOUT

1 What problems might have been encountered in re-testing original witnesses after seven weeks and how might these have affected the results?

2 Witnesses were asked to rate their confidence in what they could remember. In what way might this be important?

3 Some participants 'failed to make any identification'. Is it desirable to force all participants to make a choice? You should consider this in terms of realism and in terms of obtaining a result from the study.

4 What statistical test might have served for analysing the data in Figure 4.3? Why?

5 The extent to which an experimental procedure reflects real life is called ecological validity. To what extent does the experiment described here have such validity?

6 Part of the experiment was conducted in the 'field'. What ethical objections might be raised?

7 In the second part of the experiment participants had never even seen the suspect. In what way does their behaviour mimic that of a true witness?

8 In Buckhout's television study what sampling procedure did he use? How might this have affected the results?

9 Why do you think the participants in this latter study performed so poorly in terms of visual recall?

REFERENCES

Brown, R. (1986) *Social psychology: The second edition*. New York: The Free Press.

Buckhout, R. (1974) Eyewitness testimony. *Scientific American, 231(6)*, 23–31.

Buckhout, R. (1980) Nearly 2000 witnesses can be wrong. *Bulletin of Psychonomic Science, 16*, 307–10.

Loftus, E. (1979) *Eyewitness testimony*. Cambridge, MA: Harvard University Press.

Loftus, E., Miller, D. and Burns, H. (1978) Semantic integration of verbal information into a visual memory. *Journal of Experimental Psychology: Human Learning, 4*, 19–31.

RECOMMENDED READING

Moston, S. (1990) How children interpret and respond to questions: Situational sources of suggestibility in eyewitness interviews. *Social Behaviour, 5(3)*, 155–67.

OPTIMUM SEARCH STRATEGIES

Key terms: Eyewitness testimony, eyewitness identification, perceptual set, perception and stress, perception and conformity, leading questions.

Do-it-yourself: A Suggested Design

Hypothesis   Participants in the biased condition are more likely to identify the 'suspect' than those in the unbiased condition.

Participants   Anyone.

Design   This is an independent measures experiment.

- Prepare two identical picture spreads of suspects. One is for the unbiased condition, the other for the biased condition. The latter should include one picture that is different from the others in at least one critical aspect.
- The standardised instructions should include a description of the alleged crime and should ask participants to identify the most likely suspect. You must decide about whether you will accept 'Don't know' as an answer.
- Participants should be randomly allocated to experimental groups (biased or unbiased spread).

Ethical considerations
- Since this experiment involves deception, you should take special care with debriefing, providing *post-hoc* informed consent.
- You should avoid causing any unnecessary distress, respect confidentiality and offer participants the right to withhold their data.

Controls
- Identical photographs in both conditions.
- Two conditions: experimental (biased) and control (unbiased).
- Random allocation to conditions.
- Single blind.
- Filler (distractor) questions.
- Standardised instructions and conditions.

Materials
- Picture spreads.
- Standardised instructions and debriefing notes.

Analysis
- Descriptive statistics: means, clearly labelled tables and graphs.
- Test of association: Chi-squared 2×2. Compare the frequency with which the person in the biased picture was selected in both conditions. Condition (biased/not biased) versus selection of the photograph (yes/no).
- Test of association: Chi-squared 2×6. Compare frequency of all photographs, assuming that each should be equally likely to be chosen. Condition (biased/not biased) versus photograph (one of six).

practical
five

INTERFERENCE AND CUED RECALL

OUTLINE

This is an experiment demonstrating that interference causes lower scores in cued recall. Such a decrement can be explained in terms of a lack of accessibility (cues) rather than availability. Replication requires the preparation of word lists. Participants could be tested in small groups. Ecological validity is a key issue.

INTRODUCTION

Retroactive interference or inhibition is an explanation of forgetting. When two sets of information are learned, the new memory may interfere with the former one in such a way that the original set of information can no longer be remembered as well as it was originally. The effect is strongest when the two sets of information are very similar.

The effect is typically demonstrated by giving experimental participants two lists. List A–B consists of a set of nonsense syllables, each paired with a word. List A–C consists of the same nonsense syllables paired with different words. If participants learn list A–B then list A–C, recall is not as good with list A–B because of retroactive interference. In some cases recall with list A–C may also be reduced because of proactive interference from list A–B (forward instead of backward interference).

Example lists:

	A–B		A–C	
	BEM	lawn	BEM	aisle
	TAQ	barge	TAQ	cave
	MUZ	host	MUZ	bass

[From Ceraso, 1967]

Tulving and Madigan (1970) proposed that there are two kinds of forgetting: trace-dependent, when the physical memory trace is no longer available, and cue-dependent, when the memory trace still exists but cannot be accessed; it is available but not accessible.

Is retroactive interference trace- or cue-dependent forgetting? In other words, does the second set of information physically replace the first set, making it no longer available, or does the second set compete with the first set, limiting accessibility?

the key study

Tulving and Psotka (1971) hypothesised that if retroactive inhibition is due to decay, then cued recall should not aid memory retrieval; whereas, if retroactive inhibition is due to inaccessibility, cues should enable the information to be accessed and lead to better recall.

METHOD

Participants

They were 128 high-school students who were paid for their services, of whom 77 were males and 51 females.

Design

There were six experimental conditions: condition 1 (E1) called for learning one list of words, condition 2 (E2) for two lists, and so on up to E6 for six lists. Participants were tested either singly or in groups, up to a maximum of four people in each group. They were tested after each word list on immediate recall and then, after hearing all the word lists, they were tested on free recall, and finally they were given a cued recall test.

There were six different word lists, each with 24 words. Each list had six different categories of four words (36 categories in total). All the words from one category were presented in a block, so that it was 'obvious to all but the most uninterested' participants that there was a link between that group of words. The category names were not included in the list. The words were taken from Cohen *et al.* (1957). The order of the categories within the lists was varied for different participants to counterbalance order effects.

Two groups (designated C1 and C6) acted as controls. C1 learned one list and C6 learned six lists.

Procedure

Words were presented on a television at the rate of one word per second. The entire list was shown three times, and then participants were asked to write down all the words they could remember, guessing if they weren't sure. They were given 90 seconds for each immediate recall test which was followed by the next list.

After the last immediate recall test, a free recall test (FR$_1$) was presented. The participants were given 90 seconds per list presented.

Next they spent 10 minutes engaged on a neutral activity (the Shipley–Hartford Abstraction Test). This was intended to fill the time before their free recall was tested a second time (FR$_2$).

Immediately afterwards there was a cued recall test (CR). Participants were given a sheet for each list; each sheet had the six category names on it. They were again allowed 90 seconds per list.

The control groups spent time on the neutral activity *before* the free recall tests and did all three tests (FR$_1$, FR$_2$ and CR) in immediate succession. This meant that the effect of the passage of time on recall could be assessed.

RESULTS

The more lists participants had to learn, the lower was their mean recall of words. This can be seen in Figure 5.1, which also shows that the number of *categories* recalled declined as a function of the number of lists that interfered. Participants who learned only one list were able to remember something from each category whereas participants learning six lists remembered words from only two or three out of the six categories (=40%).

The key finding illustrated in Figure 5.1 was that the number of words recalled *within* the category remained relatively constant, between 60 and 80% (i.e. a

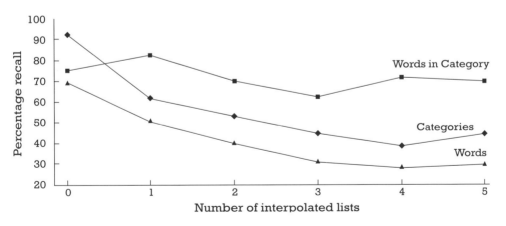

Figure 5.1 The effect of interpolated learning on the recall of words and categories (data taken from the first total recall test)
Source: Tulving and Psotka (1971). This figure and both tables copyright © by the American Psychological Association. Reprinted with permission.

mean of three out of the four words per category). This will be accounted for in the discussion.

When they were tested on free recall, participants were able to remember more words from the later lists than from the first ones (see Tables 5.1 and 5.2). This shows retroactive interference. There was no evidence of proactive interference. In fact there was proactive facilitation – recall of a list tended to be higher the greater the number of lists learned prior to learning the list in question.

On the free recall tests there was an interaction between the number of lists and performance, whereas this was only true for group E4 on the cued recall. In other words, under cued recall conditions participants were able to remember items from all lists equally well. In free recall, recall was poorer for items from earlier lists.

Table 5.1 Mean number of words recalled in free and cued recall tests for all six groups

	Group	\multicolumn{6}{c}{List number}						Mean
		1	2	3	4	5	6	
FR$_1$	E1	16.6						16.6
	E2	12.1	17.2					14.7
	E3	9.4	10.8	15.4				11.9
	E4	7.1	10.0	11.4	14.8			10.8
	E5	6.6	9.6	10.7	13.1	17.1		11.4
	E6	6.8	9.6	8.6	10.3	14.2	14.4	10.6
FR$_2$	E1	16.6						16.6
	E2	13.9	17.2					15.6
	E3	11.4	13.3	14.4				13.1
	E4	9.8	11.2	12.1	14.0			11.8
	E5	9.0	11.8	11.7	13.8	16.2		12.5
	E6	9.0	11.2	11.4	11.7	14.3	14.9	12.1
CR	E1	18.1						18.1
	E2	20.5	20.2					20.4
	E3	16.4	17.7	17.1				17.1
	E4	15.4	17.2	18.3	17.6			17.1
	E5	16.2	17.6	17.5	16.9	18.3		17.3
	E6	16.1	16.8	16.4	17.5	16.2	17.9	16.8

The recall (cued or uncued) of both control groups (C1 and C6) was not significantly different from that of groups E1 and E6. This shows that decrements in recall must be due to the interpolated lists, rather than decay over time.

One final result worth noting was that there were relatively few occurrences of words recalled that were not on the lists. The figure was highest for the cued recall (the mean per participant was 1.66).

Table 5.2 Summary of results for all groups

| | Mean number of words recalled from: | | |
Condition	First list	All lists in between	Last list
Cued recall	16.0	17.6	18.0
Free recall	7.4	11.1	15.7

DISCUSSION

The fact that words per category remained the same across all conditions suggests that access to any element of a category opened up the entire category. For example, once participants remembered the name of one bird on the list they recalled at least two other birds.

Tulving (1968) suggested that nominal elementary units (words) are organised into high-order units (categories). In order to recall a nominal unit one has to first recall the related high-order unit, even when this high-order unit was not part of the list (category name). This suggests that we access our memories in a hierarchical manner. The category heading acts as a tab – 'retrieval of one member of a high-order unit means retrieval of the whole unit'. When the high-order unit is accessed, the other contents become available. That is why cues improve memory.

Tulving and Psotka concluded that 'retroactive inhibition in free recall of organised lists represents a state of memory in which high-order units of information are available but not accessible'. Once the high-order units (categories or cues) are provided then retroactive inhibition disappears.

ISSUES TO THINK ABOUT

1 In the introduction, two explanations were offered for retro-active interference. Can you think of any other explanations?

2 What criticisms can you make about the way the results were presented? Were they easy to understand? How could the presentation have been improved? Try some alternative presentations.

3 What was the importance of the statement that the categories were 'obvious to all but the most uninterested'? How would the outcome be affected if some participants were *not* aware of the high-order category that a word belonged to?

4 How were the order effects counterbalanced?
5 Aside from order effects, what other confounding variables may have been present?
6 Why can't the cued recall task sometimes be given before the free recall task?
7 In this study, comparison on free and cued recall was among participants. Could it be arranged that one group had free recall and another had cued recall, and the results compared? What would be the advantages and disadvantages of this design?
8 Why do the data from the control groups show that recall must be due to the interpolated lists, rather than decay over time?
9 'There were relatively few occurrences of words recalled that were not on the lists.' In what way is this important? How would you deal with it if you were designing such an experiment?

REFERENCES

Ceraso, J. (1967) The interference theory of forgetting. *Scientific American, 217*, 117–24.

Cohen, B.H., Bousfield, W.A. and Whitmarsh, G.A. (1957) *Cultural norms for verbal items in 43 categories*. Storrs: University of Connecticut.

Tulving, E. (1968) Theoretical issues in free recall. In T.R. Dixon and D.L. Horton (eds) *Verbal behaviour and general behaviour theory*. Englewood Cliffs, NJ: Prentice Hall.

Tulving, E. and Madigan, S.A. (1970) Memory and verbal learning. *Annual Review of Psychology, 21*, 437–84.

Tulving, E. and Psotka, J. (1971) Retroactive inhibition in free recall: Inaccessibility of information available in the memory store. *Journal of Experimental Psychology, 87*, 1–8.

RECOMMENDED READING

Morris, C.D., Bransford, J.D. and Franks, J.J. (1977) Levels of processing versus transfer appropriate processing. *Journal of Verbal Learning and Verbal Behaviour, 16*, 519–33.

Thomson, D.M. and Tulving, E. (1970) Associative encoding and retrieval: Weak and strong cues. *Journal of Experimental Psychology, 86*, 255–62.

Tulving, E. (1979) Relation between encoding specificity and levels of processing. In L.S. Cermak and F.I.M. Craik (eds) *Levels of processing in human memory*. Hillsdale, NJ: Lawrence Erlbaum Associates.

OPTIMUM SEARCH STRATEGY

Key terms: Cue-dependent forgetting, interference, proactive, retroactive.

Do-it-yourself: A Suggested Design

Hypothesis   Participants recall more words with cued recall than with free recall.
Participants   Fellow students tested in small groups.
Design   This is a repeated measures experiment.

- Construct four word lists as described in Tulving and Psotka's experiment. Words should be written clearly on cards. The categories (cues) are written on cued recall sheets.
- Participants will be tested by showing them each word for one second. At the end of the presentation of each list, immediate recall is tested. After all word lists have been presented, free recall is tested. This is followed by a neutral activity for 10 minutes and then by cued recall, using cued recall answer sheets.
- Optional: Use two experimental conditions, with participants learning two-word lists and four-word lists. The order of presentation should be varied.
- Optional: One control condition could be used to demonstrate that time alone does not lead to spontaneous recovery of memory, i.e. people perform better on the second memory task whether it is free or cued. For this condition the neutral activity should come before the free recall test.
- Pilot study: It might help to conduct a few practice runs to work out timing and administration.

Ethical considerations
- You should remember to obtain informed consent, to avoid causing any unnecessary deception or distress, to respect confidentiality, and to debrief participants, offering them the right to withhold their data.

Controls
- Words balanced for frequency (see word lists in Appendix I).
- Order of word lists varied systematically to counterbalance order effects.
- Different experimental conditions.
- Randomised allocation to conditions.
- Standardised instructions and conditions.

Materials
- Word lists.
- Cued recall answer sheets, listing categories.
- Standardised instructions and debriefing notes.

Analysis
- Descriptive statistics: means, clearly labelled tables and graphs.
- Related test of difference: compare participants' number of words remembered under free and cued recall conditions.
- Optional use of two experimental conditions: ANOVA 2×2 (between and within subjects) Number of Lists $\times$ Type of Recall.

practical
six

LEARNING ENGLISH MORPHOLOGY

OUTLINE

This study looks at the way children apply grammatical rules to novel situations, suggesting an innate tendency to formulate and utilise such rules. Replication requires child and adult participants, and the production of a set of stimulus pictures. Participants can be tested individually. Key ethical and methodological issues are the use of children in experiments.

INTRODUCTION

The behaviourist account of language acquisition, associated with Skinner, suggests that all vocabulary and grammar are learned through imitation and selective reinforcement (shaping). In the 1950s Chomsky put forward a revolutionary concept – an innate language acquisition device (LAD). He proposed that language is learned through exposure but only because humans are born with an innate capacity to organise the input according to grammatical rules.

There is considerable evidence to support Chomsky's LAD (or language acquisition system, LAS). A good example comes from the observations of the development of sign language among deaf children in Nicaragua (described by Pinker, 1994). When the Sandinista government reformed education in Nicaragua in 1979, they created the first schools for deaf children, who until then had been isolated from one another.

During their playtimes the children invented their own sign system, which very quickly spread and became known as the Lenguaje de Signos Nicaragüense (LSN). It was an efficient communication system but not a true language because it lacked a grammar – a system of rules. However, when deaf children of around the age of 4 were exposed to LSN they developed something much more fluid and stylised, and most importantly it had a grammar. This was called Idioma de Signos Nicaragüense (ISN).

Any innate system degenerates eventually when it is not used. Therefore, the older deaf children appear to have been beyond a critical age and not able to acquire grammatical language. The younger children had a LAD, and it acted on an ungrammatical input (LSN) to yield a new and grammatical language (ISN).

the key study

Further evidence for Chomsky's hypothesis comes from an early study by Berko (1958). She demonstrated that children do not simply imitate what they hear, as had been suggested by the behaviourists, but that they learn grammatical rules and use them to generate novel, grammatically correct expressions.

Berko focused on the rules of morphology. A morpheme is the smallest linguistic unit of meaning. For example, 'toes' consists of two morphemes: 'toe' and 's'. The second morpheme denotes a plural.

The research question was 'Do children possess morphological rules?' This can be tested by asking children to apply morphological rules to novel words.

METHOD

Participants

All participants were native speakers of English. Twelve adults were tested to provide a standard against which to measure the children. Fifty-six children were tested, 10 preschool children between the ages of 4 and 5, and 46 schoolchildren aged 5½ to 7. There was a mixture of boys and girls.

Design

Participants were shown a series of cards with either new or known words and were asked to complete a sentence for each, thus forcing them to demonstrate their ability to apply certain morphological rules.

The morphological rules tested were:

- Plurals. Words tested with a picture (for example, as in Figure 6.1): glass, wug, lun, tor, heaf, cra, tass, gutch, kazh, nizz.
- Progressive. A picture showed a man balancing a ball on his nose. 'This is a man who knows how to zib. What is he doing? He is _____.'
- Past tense. A picture shows a man swinging an object. 'This is a man who knows how to rick. He is ricking. He did the same thing yesterday. What did he do yesterday? Yesterday he _____.' Other words tested: bing, gling, melt, spow, mot, bod, rang.

THIS IS A WUG.

NOW THERE IS ANOTHER ONE.
THERE ARE TWO OF THEM.
THERE ARE TWO _____.

Figure 6.1 Example card from the study by Berko (1958). This one tests knowledge of the morphological rule for forming plurals

- Third person singular. A picture shows a man shaking an object. 'This is a man who knows how to naz. He is nazzing. He does it every day. Every day he _____.' Other word tested: lodge.
- Singular and plural possessive. One animal wearing a hat, then two animals. 'This is a niz who owns a hat. Whose hat is it? It is the _____ hat. Now there are two nizzes. They both own hats. Whose hats are they? The are the _____ hats.' Other words tested: wug, bik.
- Compound forms. A picture with a man with a ball balanced on his nose. 'This is a man who knows how to zib. What would you call a man whose job it is to zib? _____.'

Altogether, participants were shown 27 cards in a 'jumbled order'.

They were also asked about compound words such as football, and asked why they thought football was called football. Other compound words used were: afternoon, aeroplane, birthday, breakfast, blackboard, fireplace, handkerchief, holiday, merry-go-round, newspaper, sunshine, Thanksgiving, Friday.

Procedure

Each child was introduced to the experimenter and told that he/she was now going to look at some pictures. The experimenter pointed to the picture and read the text. The child's answers were noted phonetically.

The entire procedure took 10 to15 minutes with each child. No child failed to understand the nature of the task. They appeared to think they were being taught new words.

RESULTS

Berko found no sex differences, even though girls are usually found to be superior to boys in language matters.

Table 6.1 shows some of the results. Significance was determined using a Chi-squared test (corrected for small frequencies using Yates's correction – though this is no longer recommended). The overall pattern was that older children were more likely to produce 'correct' answers, as we would expect, but there were many rules they had not yet mastered even at this age.

Table 6.1 Age differences in selected items

Unanimous adult answer	% of correct answers		Average % correct	Significance level of difference
	Preschool	Schoolchildren		
glasses	75	99	91	0.01
wugs	76	97	91	0.02
tasses	28	39	36	ns
zibbing	72	97	90	0.01
binged	60	85	78	0.05
glinged	63	80	77	ns
melted	72	74	73	ns
motted	32	33	33	ns
wug's	68	81	84	ns
bik's	68	95	87	0.02
wugs'	74	97	88	0.02
biks'	74	99	93	0.01

Children of both age groups were able to cope better with 'glasses' than 'tasses'. This shows some reliance on imitation, because they must be reproducing what they heard (glasses) rather than adding the plural morpheme (-es). However, the fact that older children were slightly better with 'tasses' suggests that they were in the process of learning the rule. The difference was not significant.

Performance on 'melted' and 'motted' can be similarly compared. Children of both ages performed at the same level on both, coping significantly less well with the novel word ('motted').

Looking at 'zibbing', we can see that the older children were significantly better able to cope. In fact almost all of them could produce the progressive form of 'zib'. They were significantly better able to do this (reported as $p < .05$) than to produce 'binged'. This suggests that the rule for the progressive form is learned before the rule for past tense.

The irregular verb form 'gling' posed problems for adults rather than children! Of the adults, 75% made 'gling' into 'glang' or 'glung', reflecting their more advanced knowledge that most verbs ending in 'ing' are irregular. Children, on the other hand, were happy with glinged and only one said 'glang'.

There were other results related to compound words and superlatives, but I will not report them here.

DISCUSSION

Berko comments that 'if knowledge of English consisted of no more than the storing up of many memorised words, the child might be expected to refuse to answer our questions'. The fact that children made some attempt to answer the questions shows that they had some notion of how to go about producing novel forms.

The evidence indicates that there is a consistent evolution of a child's grasp of English morphological rules. The children did not model new words on infrequent or idiosyncratic patterns but applied the most common and regular rules.

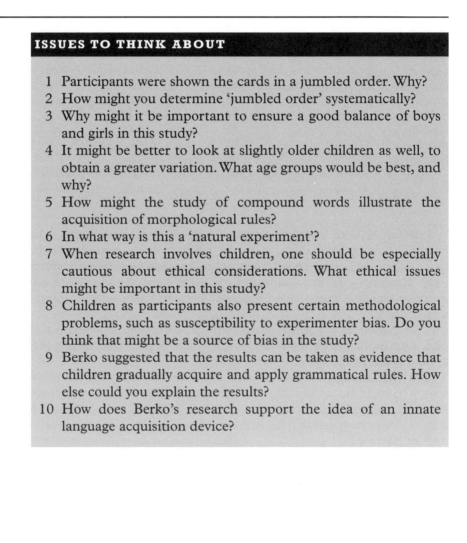

ISSUES TO THINK ABOUT

1 Participants were shown the cards in a jumbled order. Why?
2 How might you determine 'jumbled order' systematically?
3 Why might it be important to ensure a good balance of boys and girls in this study?
4 It might be better to look at slightly older children as well, to obtain a greater variation. What age groups would be best, and why?
5 How might the study of compound words illustrate the acquisition of morphological rules?
6 In what way is this a 'natural experiment'?
7 When research involves children, one should be especially cautious about ethical considerations. What ethical issues might be important in this study?
8 Children as participants also present certain methodological problems, such as susceptibility to experimenter bias. Do you think that might be a source of bias in the study?
9 Berko suggested that the results can be taken as evidence that children gradually acquire and apply grammatical rules. How else could you explain the results?
10 How does Berko's research support the idea of an innate language acquisition device?

REFERENCES

Berko, J. (1958) The child's learning of English morphology. *Word, 14,* 150–77.
Pinker, S. (1994) *The language instinct.* New York: William Morrow & Co.

RECOMMENDED READING

Brown, R., Cazden, C. and Bellugi, U. (1969) The child's grammar from I–III. In J.P. Hill (ed.) *Minnesota symposia on child psychology,* vol. 2. Minneapolis: University of Minnesota Press. There is a readable account of this in Brown, R. (1965) *Social psychology.* New York: The Free Press (Chapter 6).

OPTIMUM SEARCH STRATEGIES

Key terms: Morphology, language acquisition, LAD, imitation, grammar.

Do-it-yourself: A Suggested Design

Hypothesis   Older children apply morphological rules more often than younger children.

Participants   Two groups of children: preschool and around the age of 8. A few adults can be used to establish 'correct' answers.

Design   This is an independent measures natural experiment.

- Construct your stimulus materials consisting of cards displaying a novel or known word, and a sentence to be filled in. You can use Berko's examples.
- Establish standardised procedures, including instructions and an order of presentation. This can vary from one participant to the next to counterbalance any order effects.
- A pilot study might be helpful to practise the procedures.

Ethical considerations
- Since children are involved you must obtain informed consent from parents and from any institutions involved. Discuss your procedures with the institution beforehand. Ensure that no child participants will experience distress.
- Afterwards you should debrief all concerned parties, offering them the opportunity to withhold data.

Controls
- Order of stimulus cards varied to counterbalance order effects.
- Novel words used as the independent variables.
- Standardised instructions and conditions.

Materials
- Stimulus cards.
- Letters to describe the experiment for parents and to obtain their informed consent.
- Standardised instructions and debriefing notes.

Analysis
- Descriptive statistics: means, clearly labelled tables and graphs.
- Test of association: compare frequencies between older and younger participants using Chi-squared 2×1 test. This can be done individually for different words.
- Optional: ANOVA 2×2 (between and within subjects) Age (young/old) $\times$ Word type (known/novel).

practical
seven

DEMONSTRATING PERCEPTUAL SET

OUTLINE

This experiment demonstrated that the perception of words is influenced by prior expectations, or set. Some participants expected animal words, whereas others were 'set' to look for transport words. Members of each group were more likely to see what they expected to see. Replication involves the brief exposure of participants to a group of words and recording what they saw. A key ethical issue is deception.

INTRODUCTION

'Set' means to make something ready or to fix it (as in setting a jelly). The concept of 'set' appears throughout psychology – as cognitive set, motivational set, perceptual set and so on. Any kind of 'set' generates expectations which bias an individual's actions. Such expectations may arise internally, such as when people are hungry they are more likely to perceive ambiguous words as being related to food (Sanford, 1936). Or expectations may arise from external cues such as context. For example, Bruner and Minturn (1955) showed that the ambiguous figure **β** was interpreted as 13 or B, depending on whether it was presented in a list of numbers or letters.

Expectations may be a result of previous experience; for example, Bugelski and Alampay (1961) showed a series of animal or human pictures followed by the ambiguous drawing of a ratman. Most of them perceived the ambiguous picture in line with the set which had been generated. They were then shown the other set of pictures (human or animal). This time they did not change their perceptions. Thus subsequent experience did not alter initial perceptions.

the key study

Siipola (1935) designed a study that could be used for class demonstrations of the effects of perceptual set. The hypothesis was that set has a selective effect on the 'available possibilities of response'.

A second study explored whether set established in one situation will carry over into another.

METHOD

Participants

Six laboratory classes adding up to 180 participants.

Design of first study

Participants were shown a series of words; each word was flashed onto a screen for 10 seconds, followed by a brief interval for the participants to record the category to which the word belonged. This was either animal/bird (A–B) or travel/transportation (T–T). The words were:

- Two practice words: *ink* and *pillow*.
- Word list: *horse, baggage, chack, sael, wharl, monkey, pasrot, berth, dack, pengion.*

Four of the words were real words and the others were ambiguous – they might be seen as either (A–B) or (T–T) words. For example, *dack* may be seen as *duck* (A–B) or *deck* (T–T). The real words were included to persuade the participants to expect real words. Set was created through the instructions which each participant was given (see below).

Procedure

The written instructions for Group A were as follows:

> Ten words will be shown to you on the screen. The exposure time for each word will be very short so that you will have to watch the screen closely. Two practice words will be given to help you adjust to the task. Some of the members of the class belong to the 'naive' group and do not know what the words are about. You belong to the 'sophisticated' group, hence the following information is given to you. Most of the words you see will have to do with *animals* or *birds*. Set yourself accordingly so that you will perceive as many of the words as possible. Do not speak out the answers nor ask

questions about the words, for it is important that 'naive' [participants] get no hint as to the nature of the words. Record below in the proper order the words which you perceive.

Group T were given the same instructions, except that the words *travel* or *transportation* were substituted for the words in italic.

All the participants were misled into thinking that there was a 'naive' group, whereas, in actuality everyone was 'informed'. This deception meant however that everyone kept 'proudly silent', feeling they had an advantage over the 'poor naive' participants.

Design of second study

After a filler (distractor) activity, all participants were asked to write the missing letters in 20 skeleton words (see Table 7.1). The answers could be A–B or T–T words. For most of them there were at least 10 solutions and for some there were more than 20.

Table 7.1 Stimulus words and possible solutions

	A–B	T–T		A–B	T–T
- o a t	goat	boat	- i - e r	tiger	liner
s - - l	seal	sail	p o - -	pony	port
- - - s e l	weasel	vessel	- - e r	deer	pier
s - - - p	sheep	sloop	w h a - -	whale	wharf
- r - - s e	grouse	cruise	- a b l e	sable	cable
d - c k	duck	deck	h o - - -	horse	hotel
m a - -	mare	mast	- a r e	hare	fare
- u l l	bull	hull	- - u n k	skunk	trunk
- - b i n	robin	cabin	c h - c k	chick	check
- b - o o n	baboon	saloon	- - - t e r	setter	porter

The instructions were as follows:

Below you will find 20 skeleton words. Your task is to find real words (not slang or proper names) which can be made out of the skeleton words by filling in the blanks. In each case you are to record the *first* real word that you find fitting the requirements, and you are to see how quickly you can solve the 20 items. You are to use your pencil only in recording each word after it has been discovered; do not write anything during the process of solution. Since this is a speed test, fill in the blanks as quickly as you can.

RESULTS

Figures 7.1 and 7.2 show that participants resolved most ambiguous items in the direction of their set and that their perception of unambiguous words was also influenced by set. The actual words identified are shown in Table 7.2.

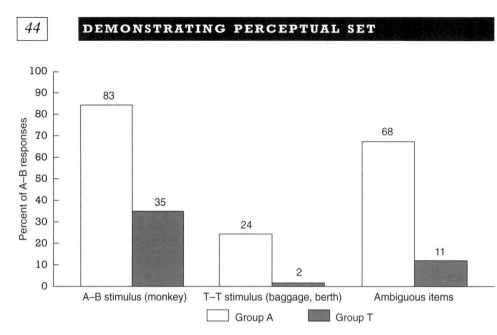

Figure 7.1 Percentage of A–B responses for each kind of stimulus item

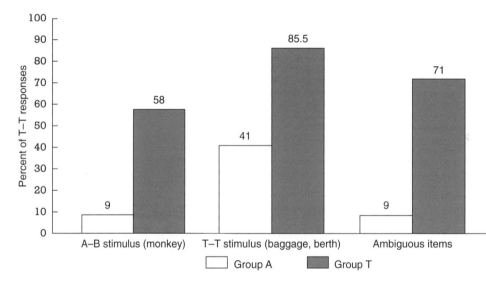

Figure 7.2 Percentage of T–T responses for each kind of stimulus item

In the second study, three times as many A–B responses were given by Group A as by Group T and four times as many T–T responses were given by Group T as by Group A.

DISCUSSION

This study confirms that set creates expectations which influence how a person perceives *incomplete* data. The real words were also influenced by set because of

Table 7.2 Most frequent responses for various stimulus items

Group A			Group T	
horse	horse (66)		horse (65)	
monkey	monkey (63)	money (7)	money (43)	monkey (28)
baggage	baggage (22)	badger (16)	baggage (54)	
berth	berth (42)		berth (71)	
chack	chick (39)	chuck (13)	check (51)	
sael	seal (45)		sail (28)	seal (16)
wharl	whale (25)	wharf (13)	wharf (46)	wheel (12)
pasrot	parrot (59)		passport (42)	parrot (20)
dack	duck (64)		deck (47)	dock (24)
pengion	penguin (38)	pension (11)	pension (43)	penguin (7)

Note: The total possible for each group was 80. Only responses occurring more than eight times are included here.

the short exposure time, creating ambiguous or incomplete data. The effects of set persisted in the second study.

The bias created by set is a necessary feature of cognitive activity because it enables us to handle incomplete data, an inevitable part of perception. The information which reaches the retina is incomplete because our heads are constantly in motion. The image is also slighlty blurred because of imperfections of the lens and the cells that lie in front of the photoreceptors. The optic disc (the point where the optic nerve leaves the eye) creates a blind spot which has to be 'filled in' by higher perceptual processes.

ISSUES TO THINK ABOUT

1 What was the point of the practice words? Were they necessary?
2 In the standardised instructions, participants were deceived about the purpose of the experiment. Do you think this was necessary and/or desirable?
3 What was the purpose of the filler activity at the start of the second study? Is this a useful technique? Does it count as deception?
4 What other techniques were employed to mislead the participants?
5 What confounding variables might have affected the study?
6 In the second study, participants were instructed not to use their pencils to write anything else. Why?

7 No graphs have been included for the second study. Would it be easier to understand the results if they had been illustrated graphically? How might you do this?
8 Siipola's article gives no statistical calculations. What test would you use on what data and why?
9 Is it possible to explain the results in a different way?
10 Do you think these results have ecological (real-life) validity?

REFERENCES

Bruner, J.S. and Minturn, A.L. (1955) Perceptual identification and perceptual organisation. *The Journal of General Psychology, 53*, 21–8.
Bugelski, B.R. and Alampay, D.A. (1961) The role of frequency in developing perceptual sets. *Canadian Journal of Psychology, 15*, 205–11.
Sanford, R.N. (1936) The effect of abstinence from food on imaginal processes. *Journal of Psychology, 2*, 129–36.
Siipola, E.M. (1935) A study of some effects of preparatory set. *Psychological Monographs, 46, series 210*, 27–39.

RECOMMENDED READING

Bruner, J.S. and Postman, L. (1949) On the perception of incongruity: A paradigm. *Journal of Personality, 18*, 206–23.
McGinnies, E. (1949) Emotionality and perceptual defence. *Psychological Review, 56*, 244–51.

OPTIMUM SEARCH STRATEGIES

Key terms: Set, perceptual set, ambiguity, perception, sensory transduction, top-down processing.

Do-it-yourself: A Suggested Design

Hypothesis   Participants are more likely to perceive a member of a category for which they have a prior 'set' than to perceive a nonmember.
Specifically, participants who expect animal words report more animal words in a list of real and ambiguous words than participants who expect transport words. The reverse is true for participants who expect transport words.

Participants   Any.

Design   This is an independent measures experiment.

- Choose your own set of real and ambiguous words or select those from this experiment. Write the words on overhead transparencies so that they can be shown to a group of participants, or on cards for individual testing.
- Add filler activities to mislead participants.
- Divide participants into two groups using a random method.
- Have independent judges assess whether answers are animal or transport or neither.

Ethical considerations

- Since this experiment involves deception, you should take special care with debriefing, providing *post-hoc* informed consent.
- You should avoid causing any unnecessary distress, respect confidentiality and offer participants the right to withhold their data.

Controls

- Words balanced for frequency.
- Different experimental conditions.
- Randomised allocation of participants to conditions.
- Filler activities.
- Single blind.
- Independent judges to assess answers.
- Standardised instructions and conditions.

Materials

- Stimulus words on overhead projector transparencies or on cards.
- Stop-watch to time exposure.
- Answer sheets.
- Standardised instructions and debriefing notes.

Analysis

- Descriptive statistics: means, clearly labelled tables and graphs.
- Independent test of association: Chi-squared 2×2, for each individual to determine whether they gave more animal or transport responses. Record preferred response (animal/transport) versus group (A or T).
- Optional: This 2×2 table could be done separately for real and ambiguous words and/or for individual words.

practical
eight

GENDER CONTENT OF CHILDREN'S BOOKS

OUTLINE

This content analysis demonstrates that certain social beliefs (representations) persist about gender. Illustrations in children's books were chosen as a means of identifying social beliefs relating to material culture – women are users of household artefacts and men use production items. Replication involves a content analysis of children's books, ideally by two judges. Collection of data requires time but no access to 'live' participants.

INTRODUCTION

Some elements of our environment are human-made. Their construction and utilisation is dictated by cultural beliefs. Such elements or processes can be called the 'material culture'. The meanings attached to material culture can be termed social representations. A social representation is the way people represent the world around them. It is based on socially transmitted beliefs which are learned through the media, parents and friends. These beliefs bias your mental perceptions.

the key study

Crabb and Bielawski (1994) focused on the fact that some artefacts of material culture are gender marked – dolls are for girls and toy trucks are for boys. They suggested that the differences between artefacts have arisen through association. In the past women worked at home and thus were associated with domestic artefacts; the artefacts became marked as female. This is a social representation.

Over the past three decades in particular more women have worked outside the home. One might therefore expect that females have become more associated with non-domestic artefacts. This would lead us to expect a change in the social representations of material culture.

One means of identifying social representations is to study children's books, especially the illustrations, because they provide specific information about how characters in the books make use of the material culture.

Crabb and Bielawski made five predictions:

Hypothesis 1: *The proportion of female characters shown using household artefacts would be larger than the corresponding proportion of male characters.*

Hypothesis 2: *The proportion of male characters shown using production artefacts would be larger than the corresponding proportion of female characters.*

Hypothesis 3: *The proportions of female and male characters shown using personal artefacts not employed in labour would not differ.*

Hypothesis 4: *The proportion of female characters shown using household artefacts would not decrease over time.*

Hypothesis 5: *The proportion of female characters shown using production artefacts would increase over time.*

METHOD

The sample

The illustrations were from American preschool books published between 1938 and 1989, all winners of the Caldecott Medal. The fact that they are award-winning books suggests that they would be popular and socially representative.

Illustrations were selected showing at least one character using an artefact ('using a human-made object to produce a desired effect'). Both the gender and artefact had to be unambiguous, and non-human characters were included.

Illustrations including architectural structures, clothing, jewellery and eye-glasses were excluded to limit the size of the sample to 1,613 illustrations. This was further reduced by following a 'proportionate sampling procedure' which ensured that the same proportions of male and female illustrations remained and that there was a proportionate representation of illustrations from the different years. The final sample comprised 300 illustrations.

Participants

Two 'Caucasian female non-traditional' students enrolled in an undergraduate psychology course acted as judges. They were not informed about the research hypotheses until afterwards.

Design

The categories were defined as:

- Household artefacts: 'Human-made objects used to produce effects in the home, including food preparation, cleaning, repair, family care and home manufacture.'
- Production artefacts: 'Objects used to produce effects outside the household, including artefacts used in construction, agriculture, transportation and all other work outside the home.'
- Personal artefacts: 'Human-made objects not employed in labour and used to produce effects on the immediate person of the user, including artefacts used for grooming, protection from the elements and leisure.'

Procedure

The judges worked independently. They were asked to assign each illustration to one of the three categories. Interjudge agreement was 0.77, which was regarded as 'excellent'. Interjudge disagreement was resolved by designating one judge as primary, determined by the toss of a coin.

Debriefing after judging showed that the judges were unaware of the hypotheses.

RESULTS

There were large gender differences in the employment of artefacts (see Figure 8.1).

Hypothesis 1: There was substantial over-representation of females in the use of household objects (using the one sample proportions test[1] $z = +5.68$, $p < .0000001$,[2] one-tailed). The one-sample proportions test was chosen because the sample was a fixed proportion of the entire sampling population.

Hypothesis 2: There was substantial over-representation of males in the use of production objects ($z = +5.88$, $p < .0000001$, one-tailed).

Hypothesis 3: There was a slight but nonsignificant difference between the male and female use of personal objects ($z = +1.31$, $p > .20$, two-tailed).

---

1 This test is described in Appendix II.
2 Crabb and Bielawski (1994) reported this level of significance. Two decimal places is usually sufficient.

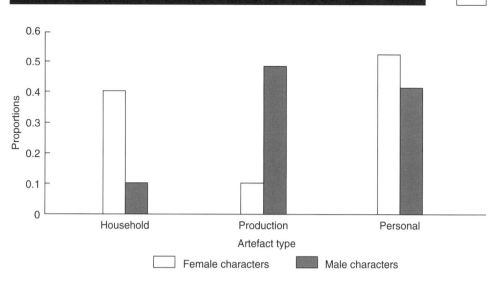

Figure 8.1 Proportions of female and male characters as a function of type of artefact used
Source: Crabb and Bielawski (1994)

Hypothesis 4: There was no decrease in the proportions of females using household artefacts over time ($z = +0.35$, $p > .37$, one-tailed). There was an increase in male use of household artefacts ($z = +4.04$, $p < .0001$, two-tailed). These data are shown in Figure 8.2.

Hypothesis 5: There was actually a slight though nonsignificant decrease in the proportion of production artefacts used by females rather than the predicted increase ($z = -1.06$, $p > .15$, one-tailed).

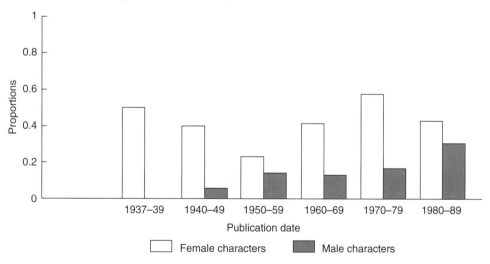

Figure 8.2 Proportions of female and male characters shown using household artefacts as a function of publication date
Source: Crabb and Bielawski (1994)

DISCUSSION

The results indicate a stable representation of gender and material culture over nearly three generations. There appeared to be some change in the area of household artefacts in terms of male use but in general change was limited, which could be interpreted as a 'cultural lag'.

ISSUES TO THINK ABOUT

1 What are your feelings about the type of sample? Does it appropriately reflect social representations?
2 To what extent do you think that illustrations in children's books are evidence of social representations of material culture?
3 Do you think it was appropriate to use non-human characters in the study?
4 What is a 'proportionate sampling procedure'?
5 The judges were 'blind' about the research hypotheses. How might it affect the research results if this was not the case?
6 How might you check that the judges were 'blind' about the research hypothesis?
7 Do you think the sex of the judges might have been important? In what way?
8 Can you think of any artefacts that would not be covered by Crabb and Bielawski's categories?
9 The conclusion was that there was no significant change over time. Do you feel that this represents the whole story as depicted in Figure 8.2?
10 Is this research interesting or useful? How might you apply these findings? Who might be interested in them?
11 What psychological theories of gender might be relevant to the discussion (or introduction)?

REFERENCES

Crabb, P.B. and Bielawski, D. (1994) The social representation of material culture and gender in children's books. *Sex Roles, 30(1/2)*, 69–79.

RECOMMENDED READING

Graebner, D.B. (1972) A decade of sexism in readers. *Reader Teacher, 26(1)*, 52–8.

King, N.R. (1991) See baby play: Play as depicted in elementary school readers, 1900–1950. *Play and Culture, 4(2)*, 100–7.

Weitzman, L.J., Eifler, D., Hokada, E. and Ross, C. (1972) Sex role socialization in picture books for preschool children. *American Journal of Sociology, 77*, 1125–50.

OPTIMUM SEARCH STRATEGIES

Key terms: Children's books, gender stereotypes, material culture, artefacts, gender development, gender bias, social representation.

Do-it-yourself: A Suggested Design

Hypotheses   As hypotheses 1–5 in the study.
Participants   Two judges.
Design   This is a content analysis of children's books.

- Go to your local library and select two samples of preschool books. One sample should be of recent books and the other of older books. You will need to think carefully about what books will be appropriate as some do not have pictures of artefacts which are gender related. You could simply use only those books which are about people. It might help to conduct a pilot study.
- You should select a proportionate sample of illustrations.
- Judges should be given standardised instructions. For each illustration, they must determine the user and note their gender and what artefact (household, production, personal) category is represented.
- Each judge should act independently. Judgements should be consolidated at the end.

Ethical considerations
- Judges should provide informed consent and be debriefed at the end.

Controls
- Standardised instructions for judges.
- Independent judgements, ideally single blind.
- Unbiased sample of books.
- Order of illustrations should be varied so that there are no order effects.

Materials
- Children's books.
- Forms for recording gender and artefact category.
- Standardised instructions and debriefing notes.

Analysis
- Descriptive statistics: means, clearly labelled tables and graphs.
- Chi-squared 2×1 test can be applied to each hypothesis using frequency. For example, for Hypothesis 1, looking at household artefacts, you could compare the total number of male and female users. For Hypothesis 4 you could compare female users of household artefacts at Time 1 and Time 2.
- Chi-squared 2×2 test could be applied to time (recent versus older books) $\times$ gender (male versus female artefacts).

practical nine

PARENTAL AUTHORITY AND SELF-ESTEEM

OUTLINE

Baumrind (1971) proposed three parenting styles: permissive, authoritarian and authoritative. This study uses questionnaires to gather data from young adults about their self-esteem and the style of parenting they received. Self-esteem was found to be positively correlated with the authoritative style and negatively correlated with the authoritarian style. Replication calls for the use of similar questionnaires. Key issues are questionnaire design and reliance on retrospective data.

INTRODUCTION

Baumrind (1971) suggested that permissive parents tend to be relatively warm towards their children; they are nondemanding and noncontrolled and tend to employ less punishment than other parents. Authoritarian parents, in contrast, value unquestioning obedience in their children and aim to control their children's behaviour, often through punitive disciplinary measures. The third kind of parenting style, authoritative, falls somewhere between these two extremes. Authoritative parents are firm, clear and relatively demanding in their dealings with their children, but their authority is flexible and rational, and the parents are willing to communicate the reasons for their demands.

Baumrind (1971, 1982) found that authoritative parenting is associated with children who are more self-reliant, independent, achievement-oriented and self-controlled than those who have experienced either of the other parenting styles.

the key study

Buri et al. *(1988) noted that the results of previous studies suggest a relationship between Baumrind's parenting styles and the self-esteem of children. For example, Sears (1970) found that where fathers were authoritarian, their sons had low self-esteem but not their daughters. Coopersmith (1967) found that boys with authoritative parents developed high self-esteem.*

Other research has found that individuals with low self-esteem tend to be less explorative and more dependent on others, to be less productive and less goal-oriented, and to have less personal responsibility and self-control.

These observations led to the hypothesis that authoritarian parental discipline is inversely related to self-esteem, while authoritative parental discipline is positively related to self-esteem.

METHOD

Participants

Three hundred and one college students agreed to participate as part of an introductory psychology course requirement. Forty-eight were excluded because one of their parents had died or their parents were separated or divorced. Another 23 participants were excluded because their response forms were inadequately completed. This left 119 females (mean age = 18.7 years) and 111 males (mean age = 19.9 years).

Design

All participants completed two questionnaires:

* The *Tennessee Self-Concept Scale* (Fitts, 1965) consisting of 100 self-descriptive items. The higher the score on the scale, the higher the individual's self-esteem. (An alternative self-esteem scale is presented on page 64.)
* *The Parental Authority Questionnaire (PAQ)* (Buri, 1991). See page 61.

Initially the PAQ consisted of 48 items. These were shown to 21 professionals (individuals working in psychology, education, etc.), who were asked to judge whether each item represented permissive, authoritarian or authoritative parenting. Only those items that received more than 95% unequivocal support were included in the final scale.

Procedure

Participants were asked to supply demographic information about themselves: their sex, their age and whether one or both of their parents had died, their parents were living together or their parents were divorced or separated.

They were then presented with the questionnaires in a randomised fashion. They were told:

- That the study aimed to investigate the family factors that were thought to influence self-esteem.
- There are no right or wrong answers and therefore you should respond to each item as honestly as possible.
- Do not spend too much time on any one statement, as your first reaction is what is required.
- Be sure to respond to all items in the questionnaires.

RESULTS

With respect to the hypothesis, we can see in Table 9.1 that self-esteem is significantly negatively correlated with mothers' and fathers' authoritarianism ($r = -.26$ and $-.18$ respectively) and significantly positively correlated with mothers' and fathers' authoritativeness ($r = .41$ and $.38$ respectively).

Table 9.1 PAQ correlations with self-esteem

	Correlation with self-esteem	Correlations for:	
		females only	males only
Mother			
permissiveness	−.04	−.03	−.01
authoritarianism	−.26***	−.29**	−.21*
authoritativeness	+.41***	+.42***	+.36***
Father			
permissiveness	−.08	−.10	−.03
authoritarianism	−.18**	−.12	−.24**
authoritativeness	+.38***	+.50***	+.19*

$* = p < .05$ $** = p < .005$ $*** = p < .0005$
Source: Buri *et al.* (1988). Copyright © Lawrence Erlbaum Associates, Inc.

For the most part the effects were similar for males and females except that there was a significantly stronger negative correlation between males' self-esteem and their fathers' authoritarianism, and a negligible positive correlation between males' self-esteem and their father's authoritativeness, whereas the opposite was true for females.

Buri *et al.* further looked at the interactions between mothers' and fathers' parenting styles by doing a median split on one variable at a time. For example, participants were split into a high or low group in terms of the variable of the mothers' authoritativeness. Those in the low group showed a weak correlation between fathers' authoritativeness and self-esteem ($r = .11$, $p < .10$) whereas for those in the high group there was a significant positive correlation between fathers' authoritativeness and self-esteem ($r = .46$, $p < .001$). This suggests that the effect of fathers' authoritativeness on self-esteem is weak when mothers' authoritativeness is low but not when the mothers' is high.

A multiple regression analysis was done on the male and female data separately. It found that:

- Of the variance in females' self-esteem, 37% was explained by the mothers' and fathers' authoritativeness, the mothers' authoritarianism and an interaction of the authoritativeness variables.
- The best equation for predicting male self-esteem accounted for 16.4% of the variance; this was an additive model of the mothers' authoritativeness and the fathers' authoritarianism.

DISCUSSION

The evidence presented here clearly supports Baumrind's distinction between disciplinary styles. We would expect from her descriptions that authoritativeness should be positively associated with self-esteem whereas authoritarianism should be negatively associated. In fact, that is what was found. Buri *et al.* suggest that authoritarian parenting creates an 'impression of limited input, circumscribed power, and restricted personal significance' that undermines the child's self-esteem. Authoritative parenting recognises the child's individuality and also maintains firm direction, enhancing an individual's sense of personal worth.

There were sex differences – males' self-esteem was more damaged by fathers' authoritarianism than females, whereas females' self-esteem was more enhanced than the males by fathers who were authoritative. Furthermore, Buri *et al.* found that the development of self-esteem in females is more dependent generally on parental authority than males.

ISSUES TO THINK ABOUT

1 The participants were all first-year psychology students. In what way may this have biased the results?
2 Some participants were excluded because they did not fill in their response forms adequately. Might this have produced a biased sample? And if so, in what way would it be biased?
3 Why were participants excluded if one parent had died or their parents were separated or divorced?
4 Would you have included or excluded children brought up by foster-parents?
5 The males in this study were, on average, older than the females. Could this affect the results? How?
6 The PAQ was validated using the judgement of various professionals. What kind of validity is this?

7 Look at the scoring on page 63. Do you agree with the designations about parental style?

8 The questionnaires were presented in a 'randomised fashion'. What does this mean? Why was it important?

9 Do you feel that the participants were deceived in any way? In what way was this desirable (or not)?

10 Some of the data were collected retrospectively. How do you think this may affect the outcome?

11 What correlation statistic would have been appropriate to use? Justify your choice.

12 What does 'accounted for 16.4% of the variance' mean and imply?

13 In the original article Buri *et al.* note one drawback to their study: that the results are based on 'nonindependent evaluations of parental authority'. What does this mean, and how might it affect the conclusions?

14 On pages 64–7 there are two self-esteem scales. What are the relative advantages of each?

REFERENCES

Baumrind, D. (1971) Current patterns of parental authority. *Developmental Psychology Monographs, 4 (2, Pt. 2)*.

Baumrind, D. (1982) Reciprocal rights and responsibilities in parent–child relations. In J. Rubenstein and B.D. Slife (eds) *Taking sides: Clashing views on controversial psychological issues* (pp. 237–44). Guildford, CO: Dushkin.

Buri, J.R. (1991) Parental Authority Questionnaire. *Journal of Personality Assessment, 57(1)*, 110–19. Mahwah, NJ: Lawrence Erlbaum Associates.

Buri, J.R., Louiselle, P.A., Misukanis, T.M. and Mueller, R.A. (1988) Effects of parental authoritarianism and authoritativeness on self-esteem. *Personality and Social Psychology Bulletin, 14(2)*, 271–82.

Coopersmith, S. (1967) *The antecedents of self-esteem.* San Francisco, CA: Freeman.

Fitts, W.H. (1965) *Tennessee self-concept scale.* Los Angeles, CA: Western Psychological Services.

Sears, R.R. (1970) Relation of early socialization experiences to self-concepts and gender role in middle childhood. *Child Development, 41*, 267–89.

RECOMMENDED READING

Hoffman, M.L. (1970) Moral development. In P.H. Mussen (ed.) *Carmichael's manual of child psychology* (vol. 2). New York: Wiley.

OPTIMUM SEARCH STRATEGIES

Key terms: Parenting style, authoritative, authoritarian, permissive, self-esteem.

Do-it-yourself: A Suggested Design

Hypotheses

1 There is a positive correlation between a maternal/paternal authoritative parenting style and high self-esteem.
2 There is a negative correlation between a maternal/paternal authoritarian parenting style and high self-esteem.
3 There is an association between a maternal/paternal parenting style and self-esteem.

Participants   Anyone aged over 16, since questions about self-esteem are involved and may be sensitive for children.

Design   This is a correlational study using questionnaires.

- Conduct a pilot study with the questionnaires on pages 61–7 to identify any problematic wording. The PAQ should be done twice, once for each parent, and analysed separately. Or you can just do it for one parent, the mother or the father.
- Prepare questionnaires with standardised instructions.
- Randomise presentation of questionnaires.

Ethical considerations

- Since this experiment involves deception, you should take special care with debriefing, providing *post-hoc* informed consent.
- You should avoid causing any unnecessary distress, respect confidentiality and offer participants the right to withhold their data.

Controls

- Randomised order of questionnaire presentation.
- Validated questionnaires.
- Single blind.
- Standardised instructions and conditions.

Materials

- Questionnaires and score-sheets.
- Standardised instructions and debriefing notes.

Analysis

- Descriptive statistics: means, clearly labelled tables and scatter graphs.
- *Hypothesis 1*: Correlation between authoritativeness score and self-esteem.
- *Hypothesis 2*: Correlation between authoritarianism score and self-esteem.
- *Hypothesis 3*: Chi-squared 2×3. Class each respondent as high or low self-esteem, and predominantly one of the three parenting styles.
- *Optional*: Look at any gender differences.

PARENTAL AUTHORITY QUESTIONNAIRE (PAQ)

Instructions

For each of the following statements, circle the number on the 5-point scale (1 = strongly disagree, 5 = strongly agree) that best describes how the statement applies to you and your mother. Try to read and think about each statement as it applies to you and your mother during your years growing up at home. There are no right or wrong answers, so don't spend a lot of time on any one item. We are looking for an overall impression regarding each statement. Be sure not to omit any items.

1 2 3 4 5	1. While I was growing up my mother felt that in a well-run home the children should have their way in the family as often as the parents do.
1 2 3 4 5	2. Even if her children didn't agree with her, my mother felt it was for our own good if we were forced to conform to what she thought was right.
1 2 3 4 5	3. Whenever my mother told me to do something as I was growing up, she expected me to do it immediately without asking any questions.
1 2 3 4 5	4. As I was growing up, once family policy had been established, my mother discussed the reasoning behind the policy with the children in the family.
1 2 3 4 5	5. My mother has always encouraged verbal give-and-take whenever I have felt that family rules and restrictions were unreasonable.
1 2 3 4 5	6. My mother has always felt that what children need is to be free to make up their own minds and to do what they want to do, even if this does not agree with what their parents might want.
1 2 3 4 5	7. As I was growing up my mother did not allow me to question any decision she had made.
1 2 3 4 5	8. As I was growing up my mother directed the activities and decisions of the children in the family through reasoning and discipline.
1 2 3 4 5	9. My mother has always felt that more force should be used by parents in order to get their children to behave in the way they are supposed to.

continued

1 2 3 4 5   10. As I was growing up my mother did not feel that I needed to obey rules and regulations of behaviour simply because someone in authority had established them.

1 2 3 4 5   11. As I was growing up I knew what my mother expected of me in my family, but also I felt free to discuss those expectations with my mother when I felt they were unreasonable.

1 2 3 4 5   12. My mother felt that wise parents should teach their children early just who is boss in the family.

1 2 3 4 5   13. As I was growing up, my mother seldom gave me expectations and guidelines for my behaviour.

1 2 3 4 5   14. Most of the time as I was growing up my mother did what the children in the family wanted when making family decisions.

1 2 3 4 5   15. As the children in my family were growing up, my mother consistently gave us direction and guidance in rational and objective ways.

1 2 3 4 5   16. As I was growing up my mother would get very upset if I tried to disagree with her.

1 2 3 4 5   17. My mother feels that most problems in society would be solved if parents would not restrict their children's activities, decisions and desires as they are growing up.

1 2 3 4 5   18. As I was growing up my mother let me know what behaviour she expected of me, and if I didn't meet those expectations, she punished me.

1 2 3 4 5   19. As I was growing up my mother allowed me to decide most things for myself without a lot of direction from her.

1 2 3 4 5   20. As I was growing up my mother took the children's opinions into consideration when making family decisions, but she would not decide something simply because the children wanted it.

1 2 3 4 5   21. My mother did not view herself as responsible for directing and guiding my behaviour as I was growing up.

1 2 3 4 5   22. My mother had clear standards of behaviour for the children in our home as I was growing up, but she was willing to adjust those standards to the needs of each of the individual children in the family.

1 2 3 4 5   23. My mother gave me direction for my behaviour and activities as I was growing up and she expected me to follow her direction, but she was always willing to listen to my concerns and to discuss that direction with me.

1 2 3 4 5   24. As I was growing up my mother allowed me to form my own point of view on family matters and she generally allowed me to decide for myself what I was going to do.

1 2 3 4 5   25. My mother has always felt that most problems in society would be solved if we could get parents to strictly and forcibly deal with children when they don't do what they are supposed to as they are growing up.

continued

1 2 3 4 5	26. As I was growing up my mother often told me exactly what she wanted me to do and how she expected me to do it.
1 2 3 4 5	27. As I was growing up my mother gave me clear direction for my behaviours and activities, but she was also understanding when I disagreed with her.
1 2 3 4 5	28. As I was growing up my mother did not direct the behaviours, activities and desires of the children in the family.
1 2 3 4 5	29. As I was growing up I knew what my mother expected of me in the family and she insisted that I conform to those expectations simply out of respect for her authority.
1 2 3 4 5	30. As I was growing up, if my mother made a decision in the family that hurt me, she was willing to discuss that decision with me and to admit it if she had made a mistake.

Scoring

Permissive parenting style is represented by 10 questions:
   1, 6, 10, 13, 14, 17, 19, 21, 24, 28.

Authoritarian style is represented by 10 questions:
   2, 3, 7, 9, 12, 16, 18, 25, 26, 29.

Authoritative style is represented by 10 questions:
   4, 5, 8, 11, 15, 20, 22, 23, 27, 30.

The scale is administered for the mother and the father, yielding six separate scores: mother's permissiveness, mother's authoritarianism, mother's authoritativeness, and then the same for the father. Each score varies between a minimum of 10 and a maximum of 50.

Source: J.R. Buri (1991) Parental Authority Questionnaire. *Journal of Personality Assessment, 57(1)*, 110–19. Mahwah, NJ: Lawrence Erlbaum Associates.

SELF-ESTEEM QUESTIONNAIRE I

This is a self-administered test that takes about 12 minutes. Alternatively, statements can be read out.

Instructions

On this page you will find a list of statements about feelings. If a statement describes how you usually feel, put a cross (X) in the column 'LIKE ME'. If the statement does not describe how you usually feel, put a cross in the column 'UNLIKE ME'. There are no right or wrong answers. For example, 'I am a hard worker, like me or unlike me?' There are 58 statements to be answered. Mark every statement.

N.B. The abbreviations on the left and the crosses in answers should be excluded when the inventory is presented to participants. They are for scoring.

			like me	unlike me
GS	1.	I spend a lot of my time day dreaming.	( )	(X)
GS	2.	I'm pretty sure of myself.	(X)	( )
GS	3.	I often wish I were someone else.	( )	(X)
SSP	4.	I'm easy to like.	(X)	( )
HP	5.	My parents and I have a lot of fun together.	(X)	( )
L	6.	I never worry about anything.	( )	( )
SA	7.	I find it hard to talk in front of the class.	( )	(X)
GS	8.	I wish I were younger.	( )	(X)
GS	9.	There are lots of things I'd change about myself if I could.	( )	(X)
GS	10.	I can make up my mind without too much trouble.	(X)	( )
SSP	11.	I'm a lot of fun to be with.	(X)	( )
HP	12.	I get easily upset at home.	( )	(X)
L	13.	I always do the right thing.	( )	( )
SA	14.	I'm proud of my school work.	(X)	( )
GS	15.	Someone always has to tell me what to do.	( )	(X)
GS	16.	It takes me a long time to get used to anything new.	( )	(X)
GS	17.	I'm often sorry for the things that I do.	( )	(X)
SSP	18.	I'm popular with kids of my own age.	(X)	( )

continued

			like me	unlike me
HP	19.	My parents usually consider my feelings.	(X)	( )
L	20.	I'm never unhappy.	( )	( )
SA	21.	I'm doing the best work I can.	(X)	( )
BS	22.	I give in very easily.	( )	(X)
GS	23.	I can usually take care of myself.	(X)	( )
GS	24.	I'm pretty happy.	(X)	( )
SSP	25.	I would rather play with children younger than me.	( )	(X)
HP	26.	My parents expect too much of me.	( )	(X)
L	27.	I like everyone I know.	( )	( )
SA	28.	I like to be called on in class.	(X)	( )
GS	29.	I understand myself.	(X)	( )
GS	30.	It's pretty tough to be me.	( )	(X)
GS	31.	Things are all mixed up in my life.	( )	(X)
SSP	32.	Kids usually follow my ideas.	(X)	( )
HP	33.	No one pays much attention to me at home.	( )	(X)
L	34.	I never get scolded.	( )	( )
SA	35.	I'm not doing as well at school as I'd like to.	( )	(X)
GS	36.	I can make up my mind and stick to it.	(X)	( )
GS	37.	I really don't like being a boy/girl.	( )	(X)
GS	38.	I have a low opinion of myself.	( )	(X)
SSP	39.	I don't like to be with other people.	( )	(X)
HP	40.	There are many times when I'd like to leave home.	( )	(X)
L	41.	I'm never shy.	( )	( )
SA	42.	I often feel upset at school.	( )	(X)
GS	43.	I often feel ashamed of myself.	( )	(X)
GS	44.	I'm not as nice looking as most people.	( )	(X)
BS	45.	If I have something to say I usually say it.	(X)	( )
SSP	46.	Kids pick on me very often.	( )	(X)
HP	47.	My parents understand me.	(X)	( )
L	48.	I always tell the truth.	( )	( )
SA	49.	My teacher makes me feel I'm not good enough.	( )	(X)
S	50.	I don't care what happens to me.	( )	(X)
GS	51.	I'm a failure.	( )	(X)
GS	52.	I get easily upset when I'm scolded.	( )	(X)
SSP	53.	Most people are better liked than I am.	( )	(X)
HP	54.	I usually feel as if my parents are pushing me.	( )	(X)
L	55.	I always know what to say to people.	( )	( )
SA	56.	I often get discouraged at school.	( )	(X)
GS	57.	Things don't usually bother me.	(X)	( )
GS	58.	I can't be depended on.	( )	(X)

Scoring

Award two points for every answer in the same position as an 'X'. Exclude lie scale items (L), which can be reported separately to indicate a person's social desirability bias.

The maximum score is 100. A score of over 75 indicates high self-esteem, a score of fewer than 25 indicates low self-esteem.

The abbreviations on the left indicate sub-scales: general self (GS), social self/peers (SSP), home/parents (HP), school/academic (SA) and lie scale (L).

Norms:
For preadolescents aged 9–15 the mean is 70.15.
For young adults aged 16–23 the mean is 76.1.

Distribution is generally skewed towards high self-esteem. The standard deviations should be between 11 and 13. A major problem is high correlations with social desirability.

Source: S. Coopersmith (1967), The Self-Esteem Institute, 936-G Dewing Avenue, Lafayette, CA 94549, USA.

SELF-ESTEEM
QUESTIONNAIRE II

Positive responses (indicating low self-esteem) are indicated by asterisks.

		Strongly agree	Agree	Disagree	Strongly disagree
1.	I feel that I'm a person of worth.			*	*
2.	I feel that I have a number of good qualities.			*	*
3.	All in all, I am inclined to feel that I am a failure.	*	*		
4.	I am able to do things as well as most other people.			*	*
5.	I feel I do not have much to be proud of.	*	*		
6.	I take a positive attitude towards myself.			*	*
7.	On the whole, I am satisfied with myself.			*	*
8.	I wish I could have more respect for myself.	*	*		
9.	I certainly feel useless at times.	*	*		
10.	At times I think I am no good at all.	*	*		

Source: Rosenberg, M. (1989) *Society and the adolescent self-image*. University Press of New England.

practical
ten

TWO MORAL ORIENTATIONS

OUTLINE

This study relies on content analysis of real-life moral dilemmas to identify a person's moral orientation(s). It was found that most people have both 'care' and 'justice' orientations but that there is an association with gender – women prefer care and men tend towards justice. Replication calls for conducting interviews and analysing the results. A key issue is the methodology associated with interviews.

INTRODUCTION

Piaget (1932) and Kohlberg (1978) have both written highly influential cognitive-developmental accounts of moral development. Both used moral stories, or dilemmas, to provide insights into the way people think about moral problems. They asked people to comment on the reasons for their moral decisions, in relation to the dilemmas presented, and used these reasons to construct stage theories of the development of moral reasoning. Kohlberg's account was the more elaborate and asserted that moral development proceeded through a fixed sequence of six stages – some individuals never reach stage 6, but everyone goes through the same invariant sequence.

A major criticism of Kohlberg's empirical work, and the theory derived from it, is that it was gender biased – the original sample included only males. A second criticism was that the theory was grounded in hypothetical rather than real-life dilemmas, which might mean that the stages lacked ecological validity.

Gilligan (1982) overcame these objections in a study where 29 women were interviewed at the time they were facing a real-life dilemma, about whether or not to have an abortion. She analysed the interviews and concluded that people rely on two different moral injunctions: not to treat others unfairly and not to turn away from someone in need (a 'justice' and a 'care' orientation). Gilligan suggested that Kohlberg's research was constrained by the assumption that there is only one moral perspective, that of justice. The alternative, care, is observed mainly by women, who tend to be concerned more about people's feelings than about what is 'fair'.

Gilligan developed her own stage theory from her interview analyses. In Stage 1 she suggested that the least mature individuals reasoned in terms of *self-interest*. Stage 2 was *self-sacrifice*, where people sacrificed their own concerns to the welfare of others. The final stage was one of *nonviolence*, where people tried to avoid hurting anyone. This is a post-conventional stage, as were Kohlberg's stages 5 and 6, in the sense that individuals have developed their own morals and are not adhering to those laid down by conventions.

Gilligan's stages can be applied to both justice and care perspectives, as seen in Table 10.1.

Table 10.1 A summary of Gilligan's three stages of moral development in terms of both justice and care perspectives

Stage	Justice	Care
1	(1J) Uphold moral standards and withstand pressure to deviate.	(1C) Concern with what others say and how choices might affect relationships.
2	(2J) Justice should be tempered with mercy. One should consider the feelings of others but principles are most important.	(2C) Sacrificing one's own concerns to the welfare of others. Relationships are more important than conventional rules.
3	(3J) While there are 'exceptions to the rule', everyone is best served by obedience to universal laws.	(3C) Attempting to apply moral rules while valuing the individual and trying not to hurt anyone.

the key study

Gilligan and Attanucci (1988) tested the hypothesis that moral reasoning can be classed in terms of care as well as justice, and that there are sex differences in these two different moral perspectives. Specifically, Gilligan and Attanucci expected that female participants would favour a care orientation and males would favour a justice orientation.

A key feature of the study was that moral reasoning was to be tested in the context of real-life dilemmas, providing greater ecological validity.

METHOD

Participants

Forty-six men and 34 women (N = 80) aged between 14 and 77. Thirty-nine of the participants were first-year medical students, of whom about half were from minority groups. Twenty of the other participants came from private high schools.

Design

Participants were asked a set of questions about moral conflict and choice:

1 Have you ever been in a situation of moral conflict where you had to make a decision but weren't sure what was the right thing to do?
2 Could you describe the situation?
3 What were the conflicts for you in that situation?
4 What did you do?
5 Do you think it was the right thing to do?
6 How do you know?

The interviewer asked other questions to encourage the participants to elaborate and clarify their responses, such as saying, 'Anything else?' Special focus was on asking participants to explain the meaning of key terms such as 'responsibility', 'fair' and 'obligation'.

Procedure

Each participant was interviewed individually for approximately two hours, including general questioning about morality and identity as well as the specific questions listed above. The interviews were tape-recorded and later transcribed.

The dilemmas were analysed using the 'Lyons procedure' as described in the Lyons Manual for Coding Real-Life Dilemmas (Lyons, 1983). This is a kind of content analysis and requires intensive training.

To maintain reliability and validity these points were followed:

• There were three coders (who showed a mean 80% agreement).
• The coders were blind to the gender, race and age of participants.
• Each dilemma was coded on the basis of at least four 'considerations' (see below). The maximum was 17 considerations.

The dilemmas were then classified as: care only, care focus (more than 75% care considerations), care justice (less than 75% of either), justice focus, justice only.

Data analysis

The coder looked at what the participant had said in discussing their moral problem. This was broken down into 'considerations', where a consideration was one argument or considered view. For example, the following paragraph from Gilligan and Attanucci described one student's dilemma about whether to inform on someone who had violated an alcohol rule. The brackets identify each 'consideration':

> [The conflict was that by all rights she should have been turned into the honour board for violation of the alcohol policy.] [I liked her very much.] [She is extremely embarrassed and upset. She was contrite, she wished she had never done it. She had all the proper levels of contriteness and guilt and] [I was supposed to turn her in and didn't.]

Gilligan and Attanucci classed this as 2J, 'a clear example of justice tempered with mercy'. Each consideration is related to principles of right and wrong, not what is best for the individual. Compare this with the following account:

> [It might just be his business if he wants to get drunk every week or it might be something that is really a problem and that should be dealt with professionally; and to be concerned about someone without antagonising them or making their life more difficult than it had to be; maybe there was just no problem there.] [I guess in something like a personal relationship with a proctor you just don't want to go out there and antagonise people, because that person will go away and if you destroy any relationship you have, I think you have lost any chance of doing anything for a person.]

In this case the speaker is focusing on how 'informing' would affect the individual and his/her relationships; he/she is more concerned with maintaining the relationship (2C) rather than maintaining rules (2J).

The following pair of considerations was given by Gilligan and Attanucci to illustrate 1J and 1C respectively:

> [If people were taking drugs and I wasn't the only one who wasn't I would feel it was stupid, I know for me what is right is right and what's wrong is wrong . . . it's like a set of standards I have.]

> [If there was one person it would be a lot easier to say no, I could talk to her, because there wouldn't be seven others to think about. I do think about them, you know, and wonder what they say about me and what it will mean . . . I made the right decision not to because my real friends accepted my decision.]

In the first of this pair the individual is concerned with right and wrong as opposed to how the others might feel, whereas in the second the individual cares about what the others think. The references in both passages are all to self-interest rather than to any general benefit to society, which is why they are both classed as Stage 1.

Finally, Gilligan and Attanucci give two examples of 3J and 3C respectively:

> [I have moral dilemmas all the time, but I have no problem solving them usually. I usually resolve them according to my internal morality. . . . The more important publicly your office is, the more important it is that you *play by the rules* because society hangs together by the rules and in my view, if you cheat on them, even for a laudatory purpose, eventually you break the rules down, because it is impossible to draw any fine lines.]

[I have to preside over these decisions and try to make them as non-disastrous as possible for the people who are most vulnerable. The fewer games you play the better, because you are really dealing with issues that are the very basis to people's day-to-day well-being, and it's people's feelings, people's potential for growth, and you should do everything in your power to smooth it.]

These illustrate the balance between following the rules, even where there are 'fine lines' (3J), and focusing on the individual and his/her 'potential for growth' (3C). Both of these individuals display post-conventional reasoning and are therefore at Stage 3.

RESULTS

From Table 10.2 we can see that 69% of the participants had both orientations (those classed as care focus, care justice and justice focus). We can also see that 66% were biased in one or the other direction (care only, care focus, justice only, justice focus) and that these biases were gender related – women tended towards care whereas men tended towards justice. If only males had participated in the study, as in Kohlberg's research, then the care perspective could have been easily overlooked.

To test the gender bias a Chi-squared test was performed on the combined data for care only/care focus, justice only/justice focus and care justice. This was necessary in order to have frequencies greater than five and thus satisfy the requirements for the Chi-squared test. For two degrees of freedom, $N = 80$, $\chi^2 = 18.33$ ($p < .001$).

Table 10.2 Frequency of moral orientations for all participants and by gender

	Care only	Care focus	Care justice	Justice focus	Justice only
All	5 (6%)	8 (10%)	27 (34%)	20 (25%)	20 (25%)
Women	5 (15%)	7 (20%)	12 (35%)	6 (18%)	4 (12%)
Men	0 (0%)	1 (2%)	15 (35%)	14 (30%)	16 (35%)

Source: Reprinted from Gilligan and Attanucci (1988) by permission of the Wayne State University Press

DISCUSSION

The results support the view that individuals tend to have predominantly one or the other orientation (care or justice) and that there is an association between moral orientation and gender. The commonest approach is a mixed one, though inevitably there is tension between the two orientations. Perhaps the greatest moral maturity is represented by those individuals who best manage to synthesise the two competing principles.

It is possible that those participants who presented only one orientation were in some way biased by the interviewers, or it might be that some respondents were reluctant to admit uncertainty and therefore preferred to answer exclusively in terms of one orientation. To overcome these problems Gilligan and Attanucci suggested that future researchers might start with the assumption that people have both perspectives and encourage a mixed response from participants, for example, by saying, 'Is there another way to think about this problem?'

ISSUES TO THINK ABOUT

1 Do you feel that there are ethical objections to Gilligan's original (1982) study? What might they be?

2 How do you think the age profile of the sample may have affected the results?

3 Do you think other participant variables may have affected the results, such as ethnicity and schooling?

4 What ethical issues might concern someone given the task of supervising the study by Gilligan and Attanucci?

5 The coding technique requires intensive training. What problems would an untrained individual have in analysing interview data?

6 What problems would occur if the data were collected in a written interview rather than in a face-to-face one?

7 What specific information about the study, and the participants, would it be desirable to withhold from interviewers and coders?

8 Do you think it would bias the outcome if respondents knew the purpose of the study? Would that be ethically preferable?

9 Gilligan and Attanucci are both women. Do you feel their account is also gender biased?

10 You could replicate this study by constructing some pre-determined moral dilemmas to exemplify the care and justice orientations. What would be the relative advantages/disadvantages of this approach?

REFERENCES

Gilligan, C. (1982) *In a different voice: Psychological theory and women's development.* Cambridge, MA: Harvard University Press.

Gilligan, C. and Attanucci, J. (1988) Two moral orientations: Gender differences and similarities. *Merrill-Palmer Quarterly, 34,* 223–37.

Kohlberg, L. (1978) Revisions in the theory and practice of moral development. *Directions for Child Development, 2,* 83–8.

Lyons, N. (1983) Two perspectives: On self, relationships, and morality. *Harvard Educational Review, 53,* 125–45.

Piaget, J. (1932) *The moral judgement of the child.* Harmondsworth: Penguin.

RECOMMENDED READING

Eisenberg, N., Miller, P.A., Shell, R., McNalley, S. and Shea, C. (1991) Prosocial development in adolescence: A longitudinal study. *Developmental Psychology, 27,* 849–57.

Discourse analysis is different to content analysis – discourse analysis looks at underlying meanings in a particular text whereas content analysis explores patterns in the text. For a readable account of discourse analysis you might look at Curtis, A. (1997) Discourse analysis. *Psychology Review, 4(1),* 23–5.

OPTIMUM SEARCH STRATEGIES

Key terms: Moral reasoning, care orientation, justice orientation, gender bias, alpha bias, beta bias, androcentric research, feminist psychology.

Do-it-yourself: A Suggested Design

Hypothesis   There is an association between moral orientation and gender: female participants favour a care orientation whereas male participants favour a justice orientation.

Participants   Aged 14 or over.

Design   This is a natural experiment using content analysis and interviews.

- Decide on a list of questions to ask your participants.
- Decide on ways of further eliciting information while avoiding the introduction of interviewer bias. Interviewers will probably not be 'blind' and therefore may influence responses. One approach might be to use a fixed set of questions with written answers.
- It would be desirable to have more than one coder to compare their analyses.
- It is not necessary to class considerations by stages. Only care/justice orientations need to be assigned.

Ethical considerations

- Since this experiment involves deception, you should take special care with debriefing, providing *post-hoc* informed consent.
- You should avoid causing any unnecessary distress, respect confidentiality and offer participants the right to withhold their data.

Controls

- Independent interviewers and judges.
- Single blind, or double blind if possible.
- Standardised instructions and conditions.

Materials

- Predetermined questions.
- Standardised instructions and debriefing notes.

Analysis

- Descriptive statistics: means, clearly labelled tables and graphs.
- Test of association: Chi-squared $2 \times 3/5$: gender versus moral orientation (care only and care focus can be combined or treated separately).

practical eleven

BIRTH ORDER, FAMILY SIZE AND IQ

OUTLINE

This study demonstrates a convincing correlation between both family size and birth order on the one hand and IQ on the other. It may be that larger families and later-born children have to share resources and therefore receive less stimulation, leading to lower IQs. This supports the view that IQ is influenced by experience (nurture). Replication involves the use of IQ tests. A key issue is the ethics of psychometric testing.

INTRODUCTION

Some curious effects have been found to be associated with birth order. With respect to personality, it has been found that later-born children are more popular among their peers than first-borns, possibly because they have to learn to co-operate with older and more dominant siblings, and this helps with peer interactions (Shaffer, 1993). First-borns are also more likely to develop leadership skills because they are given roles of responsibility for younger children (Dunn, 1984). Newson and Newson (1970) found that parents were more rigid with their first-born child, which may explain why first-borns tend to be more prone to feelings of guilt, more dependent on others, less aggressive and more conformist (Mussen *et al.*, 1984). This was illustrated in a study based on archival data (Sulloway, 1996), which found that the majority of scientists who publicly opposed the theory of evolution between 1750 and 1870 were first-borns, whereas 90% of the nonconformists, including Charles Darwin and Alfred Russel Wallace, were later-borns. Sulloway notes that Margaret Thatcher is also a later-born.

In spite of such evidence, the effects of birth order on personality have not been found to be straightforward or consistent. The effects on intelligence are more convincing. On average, first-borns have higher intelligence and achieve more in education and career. The same is true for only children (singletons).

Explanations for the determinants of intelligence are polarised between 'nature' (heredity) and 'nurture' (environment). The existence of birth order effects would support the latter view.

the key study

Belmont and Marolla (1973) noted that an alternative explanation for the apparent correlation between birth order and IQ is the intervening variable of family size. Children who are born third or fourth are more likely to come from larger families than those born second, so it might be that family size is the causal factor rather than birth order per se. It is certainly true that children from larger families tend to do less well on IQ tests, even when social class is controlled.

This study set out to examine two questions:

1 Whether there are birth order effects that are independent of family size.
2 Whether there are family size effects that are independent of birth order position.

METHOD

Participants

Four hundred thousand Dutch men were tested when they were examined for military service at age 19. The original intention of this study was to look at the effects of the famine of 1944–5 on a cohort of men born between 1944 and 1947.

Design

Dutch military examinations included tests measuring their abilities in language, arithmetic, mechanical comprehension, perceptual speed and nonverbal intelligence. Data were also collected on social factors such as father's occupation at the time of the military examination, number of children in the family and birth order position.

Nonverbal intelligence was tested with the Raven Progressive Matrices and scores were grouped into six classifications, where 1 was high. Raven scores were available for 386,336 individuals.

Procedure

Family size and birth order were each classified into nine categories, with 1–8 representing one to eight in family size or a birth order of first to eighth. A classification of 9 indicated a family size of more than eight or a birth order position beyond eighth.

The father's occupation was represented as one of three categories:

- *Non-manual*: Professional and white collar workers.
- *Manual*: Skilled, semiskilled and unskilled workers.
- *Farm*: Farmers and farm labourers.

RESULTS

Table 11.1 shows the distribution of family size and birth order, demonstrating that there were very few one-child families (5%) and that the modal group was three children. The majority of participants were first-borns, and 75% of those tested were first, second or third in birth order.

Table 11.1 Percent distribution by family size and by birth order for 19-year-old males born in the Netherlands between 1944 and 1947

No. children in family	% of total	Birth order	% of total
1	5.0	1	31.4
2	16.8	2	26.2
3	19.2	3	17.6
4	16.4	4	9.9
5	12.2	5	5.4
6	8.9	6	3.1
7	6.4	7	1.8
8	4.5	8	1.1
>8	8.5	>8	1.5
Unknown	2.0	Unknown	2.1

Source: All tables and figures reprinted with permission from Belmont and Marolla (1973). Copyright 1973 American Association for the Advancement of Science.

Table 11.2 Mean family size and birth order for each Raven class score: 1 is high and 6 is low

Raven class score	% population with class score	Family size by class score		Birth order by class score	
		Mean	SD	Mean	SD
1	18.8	4.0	2.1	2.3	1.5
2	30.1	4.3	2.2	2.5	1.7
3	21.3	4.5	2.3	2.6	1.8
4	14.3	4.6	2.3	2.8	1.9
5	10.4	4.9	2.4	3.0	2.0
6	5.0	5.1	2.4	3.1	2.0

Table 11.2 shows the mean family size and mean birth order for each of the six Raven classifications. The data show that, as test scores became lower, mean family size and birth order became higher. The same results are shown in Figure 11.1, illustrating the negative correlation.

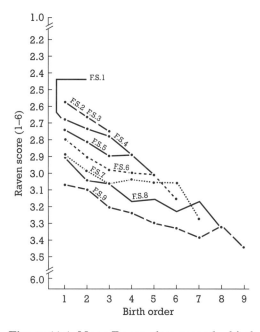

Figure 11.1 Mean Raven class score by birth order within family size (F.S.) across the population
Source: Belmont and Marolla (1973)

An analysis of birth order independent of family size showed that birth order alone could account for decreases in intelligence. In other words, no matter what the family size, first-borns do better. The same was true for family size alone, which was shown to be negatively correlated with IQ for all children in the family, regardless of position of birth.

Finally the relationship between social class and family size/birth was examined (Figure 11.2). Looking at family size first, one can see that in non-manual labourer families there is no clear negative correlation between family size and IQ and that in the farm families there is even less. The birth order effects were consistent in all three occupational groups.

DISCUSSION

The results indicate a strong negative correlation between both birth order and family size and IQ. The effects were shown to be independent because they held true when one was looking at birth order and IQ alone, and family size and IQ

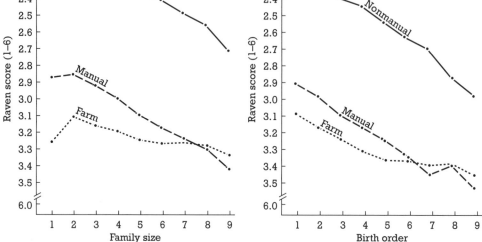

Figure 11.2 Mean Raven score for the three social class groups by family size and birth order
Source: Belmont and Marolla (1973)

alone. Furthermore, it was found that the effects of family size were not present in all social classes.

Zajonc and Markus (1975) explained the birth order effects in terms of a 'confluence model': the intellectual climate of the home is enhanced by older members and diminished by younger members. First-born children receive a greater amount of parental time, and parents have higher expectations of them, whereas subsequent children have to share attention and family resources.

This effect may be peculiar to middle-class, non-manual labourer families and to Western cultures where families live on their own. In other countries even first-born children have to share with members of an extended family and small families may be a fact on paper but not in reality.

In general, the results support the notion that IQ development can be related to experiential factors.

ISSUES TO THINK ABOUT

1 All the participants were males. They were also all Dutch. How may this have affected the results?
2 The participants belonged to a very narrow cohort. Could this have produced a bias in the results? Why?

3 What comments might you make about the occupational classification of the parents?

4 What comments might you make about the test of intelligence used? Could this have confounded the results in any way?

5 What test of correlation would be suitable for the data presented in Table 11.2?

6 Describe the birth order data in Figure 11.2. What else might you conclude from this graph?

7 The results suggest a social class difference that might be explained in terms of different cultural and subcultural ways of family life. Can you suggest an alternative explanation?

8 This study is based on IQ scores. Do you feel that there are any ethical problems associated with such data?

9 Do you think it might have made a difference if all siblings were the same sex? Why?

REFERENCES

Belmont, L. and Marolla, F.A. (1973) Birth order, family size and intelligence. *Science, 182,* 1096–101.

Dunn, J. (1984) *Sisters and brothers*. Glasgow: Fontana/Open Books.

Mussen, P.H., Conger, J.J., Kagan, J. and Huston, A.C. (1984) *Child development and personality*. New York: Harper & Row.

Newson, J. and Newson, E. (1970) *Four years old in an urban community*. Harmondsworth: Penguin.

Shaffer, D.R. (1993) *Developmental Psychology*. Pacific Grove, CA: Brooks/Cole Publishing Co.

Sulloway, F. (1996) *Born to rebel*. New York: Little, Brown.

Zajonc, R.B. and Markus, G.B. (1975) Birth order and intellectual development. *Psychological Review, 82,* 74–88.

RECOMMENDED READING

Sameroff, A.J., Seifer, R., Barocas, R., Zax, M. and Greenspan, S. (1987) Intelligence quotient scores of 4-year-old children: Social–environmental risk factors. *Paediatrics, 79,* 343–50.

OPTIMUM SEARCH STRATEGIES

Key terms: Birth order, family size, ordinal position effect, development of intelligence, confluence model, social class.

Do-it-yourself: A Suggested Design

Hypothesis   There is an association between birth position (or family size) and IQ.

Participants   Anyone.

Design   This is a correlational study, using a psychometric test.

- Select an intelligence test. Eysenck has published a book *Check your own IQ* (Penguin, 1990), containing several suitable tests. Raven's Progressive Matrices may be available through your school or college.
- Collect demographic details, including position in the family and the size of family.
- Ensure that participants are not familiar with the tests. Arrange suitable testing conditions.
- You might exclude singletons from your study, although their data could be analysed as part of a secondary hypothesis.

Ethical considerations

- You should remember to obtain informed consent, to avoid any deception or causing unnecessary distress, and to respect confidentiality. This is especially important in dealing with sensitive data such as IQ test scores.
- You must debrief participants, offering them the right to withhold their test results and any other data.

Controls

- Validated test of intelligence.
- Single blind.
- Standardised instructions and conditions.

Materials

- Intelligence test.
- Standardised instructions and debriefing notes.

Analysis

- Descriptive statistics: means, clearly labelled tables and graphs/scattergrams.
- Test of correlation examining position in family (or size of the family) versus IQ test score.
- Optional: Unrelated test of difference. Compare singletons with first-borns.

practical twelve

ELECTION CAMPAIGN COMMERCIALS

OUTLINE

This study is an example of how the content of political messages can be analysed. It focuses on the campaign advertisements of two US presidential candidates and their relative use of positive and negative messages – Bush (the successful candidate) referred to his positive record whereas Dukakis relied on ideal vision statements. Replication would call for written or visual analysis and content analysis. A key issue is the question of how the results of psychological research are applied.

INTRODUCTION

The perception you have of others is affected by the clothes they wear, the way they conduct themselves and the kinds of things they say. Snyder (1979) introduced the concept of 'high self-monitors', those people who are best at monitoring their own behaviour and adapting it to situational cues such as the effect they are having upon others.

Good self-presentation is critical in business and politics, where contracts and elections depend on conveying the right image. Psychologists are increasingly called on to analyse how such images are conveyed and to advise people on how to achieve winning self-presentation.

An example was described by Leathers (1986) in relation to a series of television debates during one US presidential-election campaign. In the first debate President Ford received higher ratings than his opponent Jimmy Carter. Carter's advisers sought advice from Leathers, a social psychologist. He studied tapes of the broadcast and concluded that Ford had used skilful visual cues to convey dominance – he stood at the lectern with his feet apart, made karate-type gestures and fixed his opponent with an unremitting stare. Carter, on the other hand, kept his eyes downcast, made few gestures and held a rigid pose. Leathers gave advice that changed Carter's style from being submissive and beaten to being Ford's equal in dominance. Carter was judged to have won the second debate and ultimately he won the election.

the key study

Hacker and Swan (1992) focused on a different aspect of campaign strategy – television advertisements paid for by political parties as a means of 'selling' their candidate. Some of these advertisements aim to promote a candidate's strengths while simultaneously highlighting the opponent's weaknesses. Hacker and Swan suggested that such advertisements have a stronger influence than other television spots because they are watched by a wider cross-section of the population than political debates and are presented in simpler terms.

The study was guided by the following research questions:

a) What messages and appeals were significantly different and the same between [the Bush and Dukakis] campaigns?
b) What messages and themes appear to be characteristic of each campaign in these spots?

(Hacker and Swan, 1992, p. 368)

METHOD

Sample

The two researchers videotaped 17 campaign advertisements in autumn 1988, and randomly selected five from each campaign for analysis.

Design

The researchers devised a coding system by watching other advertising spots. They aimed at its being 'mutually exclusive and mutually exhaustive'. Coding units were single messages (for example, a specific isolated scene, a statement about a candidate or scene). Each was classified in terms of the media dimension: oral, visual, written, candidate nonverbal (NV) and special effects. And each was classified in terms of the message appeal categories (see Table 12.1).

Table 12.1 Message appeal categories

Positive association	An appeal that associates the candidate with a figure or a scene.
Negative association	An appeal that associates the candidate with a figure or a scene to achieve an adverse effect.
Positive record	An appeal that shows what the candidate has done in his past in a positive manner.
Negative record	An appeal that shows what the candidate has done in his past in a negative manner.
Rhetorical question	An appeal in the form of a question intended to make the viewer stop and think.
Family	An appeal that shows scenes of American families or candidates' families.
Humanitarian interest	An appeal intended to make a humanitarian statement. Sometimes shows the candidate with children.
Positive trait	An appeal intended to show the personal characteristics of the candidate positively.
Negative trait	An appeal intended to show the personal characteristics of the candidate negatively.
Ideal vision statement	An appeal intended to show a candidate's ideals for his campaign which was composed largely of slogans.
Nationalism	An appeal intended to draw on the strong feelings of national pride, such as footage of past wars and pictures in which the American flag is a predominant subject.
Fear	An appeal intended to make the viewer afraid of what the other candidate will do if elected.
Positive issue position	An appeal that shows a candidate's position on a particular issue.
Negative issue position	An appeal that shows the other candidate's position on a particular issue negatively.

Source: All tables reprinted from Hacker and Swan (1992).

Procedure

The inter-coder reliability for the two researchers was 0.89. For those messages where there was disagreement they discussed them further and finally treated them as being uncodeable when no agreement could be reached.

Results

Tables 12.2, 12.3 and 12.4 display the findings.

It is interesting to note that for the Bush campaign the five most frequent categories were positive record (30%), positive trait (24%), negative association (11%), negative record (10%) and negative trait (7%). For the Dukakis campaign they were vision statement (21%), positive trait (16%), negative trait (16%), negative association (12%) and negative record (11%).

Table 12.2 Aggregate frequencies for the Bush commercials

	Oral	Written	Visual	NV	Effects	N	%
		Media dimensions				*Total*	
Positive association	0	0	7	2	1	10	5
Negative association	2	0	7	0	11	20	11
Positive record	14	18	13	0	12	57	30
Negative record	9	8	1	0	0	18	10
Rhetorical question	2	1	0	0	1	4	2
Family	0	0	0	0	0	0	0
Humanitarian interest	0	0	0	0	0	0	0
Positive trait	8	3	6	15	13	45	24
Negative trait	2	0	2	6	3	13	7
Ideal vision statement	1	3	1	0	0	5	3
Nationalism	0	0	1	1	0	2	1
Fear	5	1	1	0	2	9	5
Positive issue position	0	0	0	0	0	0	0
Negative issue position	1	2	0	0	0	3	2
TOTAL	44 (24%)	36 (19%)	39 (21%)	24 (13%)	43 (23%)	186 (100%)	

Table 12.3 Aggregate frequencies for the Dukakis commercials

	Oral	Written	Visual	NV	Effects	N	%
		Media dimensions				*Total*	
Positive association	0	0	0	0	0	0	0
Negative association	1	2	7	0	4	14	12
Positive record	3	3	0	0	2	8	7
Negative record	6	3	2	0	2	13	11
Rhetorical question	3	1	0	0	1	5	4
Family	0	0	1	0	1	2	2
Humanitarian interest	0	0	1	0	1	2	2
Positive trait	3	2	5	7	1	18	16
Negative trait	8	0	2	4	5	19	16
Ideal vision statement	10	7	1	0	6	24	21
Nationalism	0	0	1	0	0	1	1
Fear	3	1	1	0	1	6	5
Positive issue position	2	2	0	0	0	4	3
Negative issue position	0	0	0	0	0	0	0
TOTAL	39 (34%)	21 (18%)	21 (18%)	11 (9%)	24 (21%)	116 (100%)	

Table 12.4 Comparison of appeals vs. campaigns

| | Campaign | | | | |
| | Bush | | Dukakis | | |
	Mean	SD	Mean	SD	F
Positive association	0.40	1.08	0	0	3.43
Negative association	0.80	1.50	0.56	1.16	0.40
Positive record	2.28	3.70	0.32	0.90	6.61*
Negative record	0.72	1.62	0.52	1.05	0.27
Rhetorical question	0.16	0.37	0.20	0.41	0.13
Family	0	0	0.08	0.28	2.09
Humanitarian interest	0	0	0.08	0.28	2.09
Positive trait	1.80	2.24	0.72	0.61	5.42*
Negative trait	0.52	1.16	0.76	1.23	0.50
Ideal vision statement	0.20	0.41	0.96	1.67	4.88*
Nationalism	0.08	0.28	0.04	0.20	0.34
Fear	0.36	0.64	0.24	0.52	0.53
Positive issue position	0	0	0.16	0.55	2.09
Negative issue position	0.12	0.44	0	0	1.86

$* = p < .05$

DISCUSSION

The content analysis of the advertisements shows that the Bush campaign employed significantly more positive messages than the Dukakis campaign. The other significant finding was that the Dukakis campaign emphasised the visionary appeal of the candidate. These may have been perceived as irrelevant because of the insufficient number of positive messages, or it may be that many members of the electorate simply find such appeals irrelevant.

History records that Bush won the election. We might therefore conclude that the kinds of messages that Bush used are more likely to be successful.

ISSUES TO THINK ABOUT

1 Do you feel that television advertisements are a valid means of assessing election campaigns? Why?
2 What comments can you make about the sample used in this study?
3 The coding system was designed to be 'mutually exclusive and mutually exhaustive'. What does that mean?
4 When messages are coded, what problems might occur?

5 Hacker and Swan presented all their data in tabulated form, as shown here. Can you suggest alternatives? Try them out.

6 Various key factors were not mentioned in this study, such as at what point in the campaign the analysis was conducted. How might that affect the findings?

7 Are there other ways one could explain Bush's victory?

8 Are there any ethical issues raised by the employment of psychologists as advisers to election campaigns?

9 If you were advising a candidate for public office on how to conduct a successful advertising campaign, what might you say?

REFERENCES

Hacker, K.L. and Swan, W.O. (1992) Content analysis of the Bush and Dukakis 1988 presidential election campaign commercials. *Journal of Social Behavior and Personality, 7(3)*, 367–74.

Leathers, D.G. (1986) *Successful nonverbal communication*. Cambridge: Cambridge University Press.

Snyder, M. (1979) Self-monitoring processes. In L. Berkowitz (ed.) *Advances in experimental social psychology* (Vol. 6). New York: Academic Press.

RECOMMENDED READING

Meadow, R.G. and Sigelman, L. (1982) Some effects and noneffects of campaign commercials: An experimental study. *Political Behaviour, 4*, 163–75.

OPTIMUM SEARCH STRATEGIES

Key terms: Political advertising, commercials, persuasive messages, attitudes, attitude change, self-monitoring.

Do-it-yourself: A Suggested Design

Hypothesis   Candidate X uses more negative messages than candidate Y.
Sample   Party political broadcasts.
Design   A content analysis of advertising messages.

- Pilot study to develop a coding system. Adapt the system devised by Hacker and Swan for British political messages. A tool developed specifically for this hypothesis should look only at negative messages; all different messages should be classed as 'other'.
- Videotape a selection of political broadcasts so that you have a representative sample.
- Show the tapes to at least two judges (who could include yourself) and discuss decisions afterwards.

Ethical considerations
- Any judge should give informed consent, and be debriefed afterwards (for example, shown the results).

Controls
- Independent judgements, ideally blind to purpose of study. There should be high inter-judge agreement.
- Standardised coding system.

Materials
- Videotapes of political messages.
- Coding sheet.

Analysis
- Descriptive statistics: means, clearly labelled tables and graphs.
- Test of association: count frequency of negative messages. Chi-squared 2×1 (party X versus party Y).
- Optional: difference between means, one-way ANOVA. The F ratio can be used to test whether one mean differs significantly from another.

practical thirteen

MERE PRESENCE AND SOCIAL FACILITATION

OUTLINE

Improved performance in the presence of others (social facilitation) can be explained in terms of evaluation apprehension. This experiment demonstrates that evaluation apprehension alone cannot account for social facilitation effects on dominant and nondominant tasks. Replication is fairly straightforward. Key issues are deception, the use of confederates and volunteer bias.

INTRODUCTION

The first experiment in social psychology was conducted by Norman Triplett (1897), who observed that cyclists racing against each other performed faster than they did when they were practising on their own. He suggested that the presence of others created greater competitiveness, and he tested this hypothesis by arranging for children to turn fishing reels together and alone. He found that working side-by-side (co-acting) led to improved performance.

Subsequent research has identified various features of this social influence. Zajonc (1965) made the distinction between dominant and nondominant responses. The former are well-learned, instinctive, simple motor tasks that are enhanced, at least in terms of quantity of output, by the presence of others (*social facilitation*). The latter are novel, conceptual tasks where performance is depressed by the presence of others (*social inhibition*).

In situations where individuals are co-acting (*co-action effect*) or are being watched (*audience effect*) performance is enhanced or depressed in relation to whether the task is dominant or nondominant. This may be due to apprehension of what others may think (*evaluation apprehension*). It leads to increased arousal, which will enhance performance on easy tasks but not on more difficult, nondominant tasks.

It is also possible for individuals to *interact*. This may have a positive effect, as in 'brainstorming' where a group can outperform individuals in quality of ideas. On the other hand, interaction may result in *social loafing*, as in the Ringlemann effect. For example, each individual on a tug-of-war team exerts less force when they all pull together than they would pulling on their own.

the key study

Schmitt et al. *(1986) suggested that 'one of the most intriguing aspects of Zajonc's formulation of social facilitation effects is his claim that the mere presence of another person' can lead to improved performance. This is hard to understand; if an observer is not in any way able to evaluate performance then the performer should not experience evaluation apprehension.*

Their hypothesis was that the mere presence of another person increases arousal and therefore speeds up performance on a dominant (well-learned) task, but slows it down on a nondominant (novel) task.

Previous tests of this hypothesis overlooked the fact that any participant in an experiment will have a sense of being evaluated even when no observer is directly watching. In order to avoid this possibility it is necessary to make participants feel that the activity during which their performance is assessed is not actually part of the experiment. Markus (1978) did this by asking participants to prepare for an experiment by taking off their shoes (dominant task) and putting on the socks, shoes and laboratory coat provided (nondominant task). When the experiment was cancelled they had to reverse the process. Markus found that participants handled their own shoes faster than the laboratory clothes when in a 'mere presence' condition as compared with an 'alone' condition. In this experiment, however, 'mere presence' meant another person with their back turned. This wasn't the same as no awareness, and therefore there may have been a sense of evaluation apprehension. Schmitt et al. intended to rule out the possibility of any awareness in their experiment and therefore provide a better test of the 'mere presence' hypothesis.

METHOD

Participants

Forty-five male and female undergraduates volunteered to take part in a sensory-deprivation experiment.

Design

Participants were asked to give some background information before the start of the experiment. They sat at a computer and were presented with the following questions:

- What is your name? (This is the easy, well-learned task.)
- Type in a code by writing your name backwards and interspersing each letter with ascending digits. (This is the difficult, novel task.)
- Several filler (distractor) questions were included.

The time taken to do the first two tasks was recorded by the computer.

Procedure

Participants were randomly assigned to one of three conditions:

1. The 'alone' condition, where the experimenter left the participants on their own while the questions were answered, saying he would not return until a bell sounded to signal the end of the questions.
2. The 'mere presence' condition, where a confederate of the experimenter was in the room while the questions were being answered but was wearing a large blindfold and a pair of headphones and had his back turned to the participants. Participants were told that the confederate was taking part in the sensory deprivation section of the experiment. The experimenter watched through a one-way mirror.
3. The 'evaluation apprehension' condition, where the experimenter stayed in the room and peered over the participants' shoulders.
   The experiment was therefore a 2×3 factorial design, a novel versus a well-learned task under three conditions. It took approximately five minutes.

RESULTS

The deception appeared to be successful because all the participants expressed surprise when they were told that the experiment was over after the question phase. Participants also said that they were not aware they had been timed. None of the participants in the 'mere presence' condition expressed any suspicion about the confederate.

The results are shown in Table 13.1. A 2×3 repeated measures ANOVA of the data revealed a main effect of task difficulty ($F(1,42) = 170.33$, $p < .0001$) and

Table 13.1 Mean time in seconds to complete the well-learned and novel tasks

	Alone (N=15)	Mere presence (N=15)	Evaluation apprehension (N=15)
Well-learned task	14.77	9.83	7.07
Novel task	52.41	72.57	62.52

Source: Schmitt *et al.* (1986) with permission from Academic Press, Inc., Florida.

a significant interaction between task difficulty and audience condition ($F(2,42) = 3.52, p<.05$).

Mere presence of the confederate was sufficient to produce the 'standard social facilitation effects', that is, participants performing the familiar task more quickly ($t = 2.6, p = .0166$) and the novel task more slowly ($t = -2.06, p = .0511$).

DISCUSSION

The importance of this result is that it demonstrates that evaluation apprehension is not a *necessary* condition for social facilitation, though it does serve to increase the effect.

Schmitt *et al.* noted, however, that the participants in the 'mere presence' condition may have been in a state of heightened arousal because the blindfolded confederate served to remind them that they would soon be doing the same thing as part of the experiment proper – 'a prospect some of them may have found worrisome'. On the other hand, they may have been relieved to learn that the sensory-deprivation part was not going to be troublesome, in which case they would not be in a state of heightened arousal.

To control for this, Schmitt *et al.* conducted a follow-up study where all participants were told at the beginning that they would be controls for the sensory-deprivation experiment and, in the case of the 'mere presence' condition, the confederate was described as a member of the experimental group. In spite of this change, the overall results remained the same.

Therefore, the experimenters concluded that the effect is primarily due to a sense of social comparison. Zajonc (1980) pointed out that the word 'mere' may be misleading since the presence of anyone entails some recognition of a significant other and some sense of social comparison. After all, Schmitt *et al.* suggest, we would not expect the effect to occur in the presence of a non-human animal.

ISSUES TO THINK ABOUT

1 Concerning Markus' experiment, do you feel that the tasks were representative of dominant and nondominant activities? In other words, was this a valid test of the hypothesis?

2 What comments might you make on the activities (independent variables) of the experiment by Schmitt *et al.*?

3 The participants were volunteers. How might this have biased the findings?

4 What does 'the participants were randomly assigned to one of three conditions' mean?

5 In the 'evaluation apprehension' condition the effect was to make the participants feel they were being evaluated. Could

there be another explanation of why their performance might have been influenced in this condition?

6 What effect would it have on the data if some of the participants had found the confederate's presence worrisome, and others had not?

7 If any participants were not surprised at the deception, what action should have been taken?

8 Were ANOVA and the *t*-test appropriate tests to use? Explain your answers.

9 In the follow-up experiment, the experimenters arranged for all the participants to think they were members of the control group. How would that make a difference?

10 Would you expect the social facilitation effect to occur in the presence of a non-human animal? Why?

REFERENCES

Markus, H. (1978) The effect of mere presence on social facilitation: An unobtrusive test. *Journal of Experimental Social Psychology, 14*, 380–97.

Schmitt, B., Gilovich, T.K., Goore, N. and Joseph, L. (1986) Mere presence and social facilitation: One more time. *Journal of Experimental Social Psychology, 22*, 242–8.

Triplett, N. (1897) The dynamogenic factors in pacemaking and competition. *American Journal of Psychology, 9*, 507–33.

Zajonc, R.B. (1965) Social facilitation. *Science, 149*, 269–74.

Zajonc, R.B. (1980) Compresence. In P.B. Paulus (ed.) *Psychology of group influence* (pp. 35–60). Hillsdale, NJ: Erlbaum.

RECOMMENDED READING

Latané, B, Williams, K. and Harkins, S. (1979) Many hands make light work: The causes and consequences of social loafing. *Journal of Personality and Social Psychology, 37*, 822–32.

OPTIMUM SEARCH STRATEGIES

Key terms: Social facilitation, social inhibition, co-action effect, audience effect, evaluation apprehension, social comparison.

Do-it-yourself: A Suggested Design

Hypothesis   Participants in the mere presence condition perform the well-learned task faster and perform the novel task slower than those in the alone condition.

Participants   Any literate/numerate individuals.

Design   This is an independent and repeated measures experiment (mixed design).

- Tell participants that the first activity is a prelude to the experiment itself. This is the single blind.
- Repeated measures: Tasks 1 and 2, plus some filler activities. Task 1: A well-learned task such as writing your name repeatedly or doing some simple addition sums on a piece of paper for one minute, as measured by an egg-timer. When the time is up, the participants should stop and notify the experimenter. Task 2: A novel task such as writing your name in code backwards repeatedly or doing a set of long-addition sums with carrying, again timed for one minute. (If you have access to a computer and can use a mechanism for timing, all the better.)
- Independent measures: Participants should be randomly assigned to Condition A (mere presence) or Condition B (alone). You could have a third condition, evaluation apprehension.
- You should counterbalance order effects by getting half the participants in Condition A to do Task 1 first and the other half to do it second. The same should be true for Condition B.

Ethical considerations
- Since this experiment involves deception, you should take special care with debriefing, providing *post-hoc* informed consent.
- You should avoid causing any unnecessary distress, respect confidentiality and offer participants the right to withhold their data.

Controls
- Single blind and filler activities to stop participants guessing the experiment's purpose.
- Counterbalance order effects for tasks.
- Different experimental conditions.
- Random allocation to conditions.
- Standardised instructions and conditions.

Materials
- Well-learned and novel tasks, filler activities.
- Standardised instructions and debriefing notes.

Analysis
- Descriptive statistics: means, clearly labelled tables and graphs comparing the performance of both experimental groups on both tasks.
- Unrelated test of difference. Compare each group's performance on Task 1 (participants in Condition A should have done more than those in Condition B) and Task 2 (participants in Condition A should have done less than those in Condition B).
- Optional: ANOVA 2×2 (between and within subjects). Type of Task $\times$ Condition.

practical
fourteen

WEATHER, MOOD AND HELPING BEHAVIOUR

OUTLINE

This field experiment provides evidence that sunshine has a positive effect on willingness to help others. Replication calls for asking passers-by how many questions they would be prepared to answer out of a total of 80. A key ethical issue is the inevitable absence of informed consent.

INTRODUCTION

There are many factors influencing the likelihood of whether someone will help in an emergency. They relate to the ambiguity of the situation, the diffusion of responsibility and the costs of intervening. When psychologists have studied helping in non-emergency situations, they have found that other factors emerge. One key variable is the weather. For example, Lockard *et al.* (1976) found that panhandlers (beggars) were more successful in the spring than in the autumn.

Psychological research has focused on other weather effects. For example, Griffitt and Veitch (1971) found that participants' evaluations of others were more negative when a laboratory was overheated than when it was comfortable. Baron (1987) found that negative ions increased liking for someone who had similar attitudes but had the opposite effect with a stranger who had dissimilar attitudes. In other words, it intensified interpersonal feelings. Baron and Ransberger (1978) analysed records of collective violence in the US over a four-year period and found a curvilinear relationship between temperature and aggression: aggression increased as heat rose, up to a point. At over 90°F it dropped.

the key study

Cunningham (1979) pointed out that straightforward conclusions about the effects of weather are difficult when average daily records are consulted, because one cannot assume that a particular weather variable and the behaviour observed did occur simultaneously. In that case there would be no causal relationship.

One way to overcome this difficulty would be to conduct controlled laboratory studies, but obviously some weather variables, such as sunshine and barometric pressure, cannot be easily controlled in this way. To overcome this difficulty a behavioural assessment should be conducted in the field together with a simultaneous record of key weather variables.

There were a number of predictions for the effects of weather, based on earlier research:

- *A positive correlation between barometric pressure and helping behaviour.*
- *A negative correlation between humidity and helping behaviour.*
- *A U-shaped (curvilinear) relationship between temperature and helping behaviour, which will be lowest when the temperature is very high or very low.*
- *A positive correlation between sunshine and helping behaviour.*

In all of these conditions it was proposed that mood is the intervening variable:

- *Sunshine improves mood, leading to higher rates of helping behaviour.*
- *Low barometric pressure, high humidity and extreme temperatures depress mood, leading to lower rates of helping behaviour.*

METHOD

Participants

A total of 540 passers-by were questioned at four locations, two in the city of Minneapolis and two on the college campus.

Design

Fifteen participants were approached each day on 36 separate weekdays over the spring, summer and winter seasons. The interviewer stopped every third individual who appeared to be older than age 16. An average of four people per day refused to stop. Data were not collected on rainy days.

Weather readings were taken at the beginning of every hour, which included:

- Amount of sunlight, measured by a light meter.
- Lunar phase, from an almanac.
- Atmospheric temperature.

- Barometric pressure.
- Relative humidity.
- Wind velocity.
- Air pollution, for example, carbon monoxide and sulphur dioxide levels.

All measures except the first two were obtained from the National Weather Service at Minneapolis.

Procedure

One experimenter approached a passer-by with the following statement:

> Hi. I'm from the sociology department of the University of Minnesota, and we're conducting a survey of social opinions. Although the survey is 80 questions long, you don't have to answer all the questions. How many questions would you be willing to answer for me?

The number of questions the participants was willing to answer served as a measure of helpfulness. Participants were debriefed after their response. The experimenter recorded the sex and approximate age of each participant.

RESULTS

Table 14.1 shows that, consistent with predictions, sunshine and barometric pressure were positively correlated with helping behaviour, and that relative humidity was negatively correlated with helping behaviour. A curvilinear correlation was found for temperature ($p < .001$) centred on a low point of 65°F.

There were some seasonal differences, for example, temperature was more significantly correlated with helping behaviour in winter than in summer.

Table 14.1 Correlations of weather and participant variables with amount of help offered to an interviewer

Item	Correlation
Sunshine	0.36*
Temperature	0.11*
Barometric pressure	0.04
Relative humidity	−0.20*
Wind velocity	0.01
Air pollution index (Apex)	−0.02
Sulphur dioxide	−0.15*
Carbon monoxide	−0.03
Lunar phase[a]	−0.15*
Age	0.04
Sex[b]	0.10

* = $p < .001$
[a] = the highest value was given for a full moon
[b] = the highest value = a female

DISCUSSION

Helping rates were higher on bright, sunny days than on cloudy days. They were also higher during periods of cooler temperatures and higher winds in summer, and warmer temperatures and lower winds in winter.

This effect may be due to the comfort and discomfort which participants experienced. It cannot, however, explain the effects of sunshine, because in Minnesota many cloudless days in winter are very cold. Nevertheless, sunshine was still associated with a greater likelihood of helping.

In order to test a further hypothesis that sunshine is an independent factor, Cunningham assessed helpfulness in terms of the ratio of tips to the actual bill given to a waitress in an indoor restaurant. This confirmed that, when comfort factors such as wind and temperature are controlled, sunshine remains an important variable.

Sunshine may give rise to a more positive mood because of its positive associations (with picnics, the beach, etc.), or because it makes the environment brighter and more stimulating, or because it has a positive effect on physiological processes.

ISSUES TO THINK ABOUT

1 What is a 'curvilinear relationship'?
2 Why do you think experimenters only stopped every third passer-by? What kind of sampling method is this an example of?
3 The number of questions a participant was prepared to answer was the dependent variable. Do you feel this is a valid measure of helpfulness? Explain your answer.
4 Was it necessary to test participants in both summer and winter? Why?
5 What information should have been included in the debriefing?
6 Could the debriefing have biased the results?
7 Cunningham calls this a 'quasi-experimental' design. Why? (Think about the independent variables.)
8 What statistical test might have been used? Why?
9 How reliable was it to collect data from the weather centre in view of Cunningham's comments on page 97?
10 The discussion contains four paragraphs. What is the purpose of each?

REFERENCES

Baron, R.A. (1987) Effect of negative air ions on interpersonal attraction: Evidence for intensification. *Journal of Personality and Social Psychology, 52,* 547–53.

Baron, R.A. and Ransberger, V.M. (1978) Ambient temperature and the occurrence of collective violence: The 'long hot summer' revisited. *Journal of Personality and Social Psychology, 36,* 351–60.

Cunningham, M.R. (1979) Weather, mood and helping behaviour: Quasi-experiments with the sunshine Samaritan. *Journal of Personality and Social Psychology, 37,* 1947–56.

Griffitt, W. and Veitch, R. (1971) Hot and crowded: Influences of population density and temperature on interpersonal affective behaviour. *Journal of Personality and Social Psychology, 17,* 92–8.

Lockard, J.S., McDonald, L.L., Clifford, D.A. and Martinez, R. (1976) Panhandling: Sharing of resources. *Science, 191,* 406–8.

RECOMMENDED READING

Beaman, A.L., Barnes, P.J., Klentz, B. and McQuirk, B. (1978) Increasing helping rates through information dissemination: Teaching pays. *Personality and Social Psychology Bulletin, 4,* 406–11.

Darley, J.M. and Batson, C.D. (1973) 'From Jerusalem to Jericho': A study of situational and dispositional variables in helping behaviour. *Journal of Personality and Social Psychology, 27,* 100–8.

OPTIMUM SEARCH STRATEGIES

Key terms: Weather, sunshine, barometric pressure, humidity, temperature, helping behaviour, co-operation, altruism.

Do-it-yourself: A Suggested Design

Hypothesis There is a positive correlation between sunshine and helping behaviour. (You could predict and test other aspects of the weather as well.)

Participants Passers-by (an opportunity sample).

Design This is a quasi-experiment conducted in the field.

- Select various different sites to approach passers-by.
- Determine how you will select participants, how you will assess helpfulness (number of questions a participant is willing to answer) and how you will record the level of sunshine (for example, with a light meter).

Ethical considerations

- You will not be able to obtain informed consent from your participants. Therefore debriefing is especially important, offering them the right to withhold their data or supply *post-hoc* informed consent.
- You must avoid any unnecessary deception or causing distress to participants, and remember to respect confidentiality.
- If you conduct your study on private property, such as a shopping centre, be sure to obtain permission from the owner.

Controls

- Single blind.
- Samples collected in different places.
- Reducing any bias in the selection of participants.
- Standardised instructions and conditions.

Materials

- Light meter (for sunshine).
- Bogus questionnaire.
- Paper to record details.
- Standardised instructions and debriefing notes.

Analysis

- Descriptive statistics: means, clearly labelled tables and graphs.
- Test of correlation: co-variables are amount of light and number of questions the participant was willing to answer (or other measure of helpfulness).

practical *fifteen*

THE EFFECTS OF PHYSICAL ATTRACTIVENESS

OUTLINE

This experiment demonstrates some of the benefits of being physically attractive. Replication requires a set of stimulus paragraphs, together with photographs. Data collection is straightforward. A key ethical issue in the study was the deception of participants. A methodological issue was having only female students as participants.

INTRODUCTION

When you meet someone you consider to be good-looking, psychological research shows that you will probably think they have traits such as kindness and trustworthiness. Conversely, people who are considered unattractive are perceived as having 'bad' traits such as meanness and untrustworthiness (which is why 'bad guys' on television often have a large, hooked nose and perhaps an eye patch).

The *halo effect* is the tendency for people who possess one socially desirable characteristic to be assumed to possess a host of other positive characteristics. Physical attractiveness is a particularly outstanding trait, both because it is usually obvious and because it is highly influential in the process of impression formation.

the key study

Dion (1972) suggested that the halo effect already operates at an early age; for example, physically attractive children are more popular at preschool. She suggested that they have learned this stereotype, and the associated expectations, from adults. The observation that adults tend to treat physically attractive children preferentially leads to two hypotheses:

1 *'An attractive child who commits a harmful act will be perceived as less likely to exhibit chronically antisocial behaviour than an unattractive child.' Adults expect attractive children to behave in a more socially acceptable fashion. A harmful act, or transgression, would therefore be seen as inconsistent and not attributed to the child's likely behaviour in the past or the future. An unattractive child would be expected to behave in a more antisocial fashion, and therefore evidence of such behaviour would be seen as consistent.*

2 *'A transgression committed by an attractive child will be evaluated as less socially undesirable than the same act committed by an unattractive child.' This prediction also comes from the inconsistency between an attractive child and an antisocial act. In order to resolve the inconsistency the act is perceived differently. It should also mean that attractive children would receive less punishment.*

METHOD

Participants

Of 243 female undergraduates, some were psychology students who received course credits and others were sociology students who were paid $1.50. Dion argued that this sample was appropriate because 'women of approximately this age group generally constitute the primary socialising influence in the home and in the [primary] school'.

Design

There were 16 experimental conditions, hence this was a $2 \times 2 \times 2 \times 2$ factorial design. The independent variables were:

* Attractiveness of the child (attractive or unattractive).
* Severity of the offence (mild or severe).
* Sex of child (male or female).
* Type of offence (impersonal or interpersonal).

Participants were asked to read a behavioural description of a 7-year-old. This was said to have come from a teacher's daily journal reporting incidents at school, in the playground and in the classroom. Each description included the child's name, age, a description of his/her behaviour and a black-and-white photograph glued to one corner.

Altogether there were four photographs of each sex at each attractiveness level. The photographs were selected after being rated on a 5-point scale by nine judges.

The behavioural reports consisted of a brief description of the child's transgression. An example for the severe–impersonal condition:

> At one corner of the playground a dog was sleeping. Peter stood a short distance from the dog, picked up some sharp stones from the ground, and threw them at the animal. Two of the stones struck the dog and cut its leg. The animal jumped up yelping and limped away. Peter continued to throw rocks at it as it tried to move away from him.

This was varied for the other conditions:

- Mild–impersonal condition: The child stepped on the dog's tail, making it yelp.
- Severe–interpersonal condition: The child packed a sharp piece of ice into a snowball and aimed it at another child's head, causing a deep, bleeding cut.
- Mild–interpersonal condition: The child threw an ordinary snowball that stung another child's leg.

Participants were asked to make attributions about the child's personality with:

1 An attitude scale in the form of a 17-centimetre line with no markings other than 'anchor words' at either end. The participant expresses an opinion by placing a mark on the continuum, which can then be measured. The continuums measured:

- The likelihood that the child had committed a similar harmful act in the past (very unlikely – very likely).
- The probability that he would commit a similar act in the future (very improbable – very probable).
- The undesirability of the act itself (not undesirable at all – extremely undesirable).
- The intensity of punishment advised for the child (very mild – very strong).

2 Personality trait dimensions:

- Six were chosen for subsequent analysis (good–bad, aggressive–nonaggressive, pleasant–unpleasant, kind–cruel, honest–dishonest, nice–awful).
- Physically attractive–unattractive was included as a 'manipulation check'.
- Nine dimensions were included as fillers (to distract the participants).

3 Open-ended questions were included:

- Why did the child commit the harmful act?
- How did the child usually behave on a typical day?

4 Another set of questions was used to identify:

- Participants who misunderstood the questions (as a result, three participants were 'discarded').
- Participants who were suspicious about the true purpose of the study.

Procedure

Participants were randomly assigned to a condition. The instructions they were given were that the experiment focused on 'adults' evaluations of children's behaviour'. The participants were told that the experiment was for the purpose of trying to find out whether 'richer judgements' were made of behaviour when it was directly or indirectly observed. In the experiment they would be making indirect judgements. They were told to read the behavioural description and put it in an envelope, thus simulating real-life situations where judgements are made after behaviour is observed with no 'instant replay'.

No debriefing was reported in the journal article.

RESULTS

Manipulation check

It was confirmed, with an analysis of variance test,[1] that the 'attractive' children were rated as being more attractive ($F = 93.45$ and 45.31, for females and males respectively, both $p < .001$).

A second check was done to see whether the offences were rated as different and the severe offence was seen as being more undesirable than the mild one ($F = 20.74$ and 62.82, for impersonal and interpersonal aggression respectively, for both $p < .001$).[2]

There was a Severity × Type of Offence interaction. Mild impersonal aggression was rated more negatively than mild interpersonal aggression ($F = 14.37$, $p < .001$).

Attitudes

There was an interaction between attractiveness and severity of the offence. Dion performed two Chi-squared analyses,[3] one on the mild transgression condition and one on the severe transgression condition. In the mild condition there were no differences between the behavioural ratings for attractive and unattractive children ($\chi^2 = 3.30$, $df = 2$, ns). In the severe condition the differences were significant ($\chi^2 = 6.26$, $df = 2$, $p < .05$).

Trait ratings

There were main effects for the two trait dimensions 'honest–dishonest' and 'pleasant–unpleasant'. Unattractive children were perceived as being more

---

1 ANOVA tests are discussed in Appendix II.

2 In the original article the degrees of freedom (df) were not reported. Today it would be considered good practice to include this data.

3 In order to analyse the data in this study, Dion has collapsed parametric data to non-parametric form.

dishonest ($F = 9.70$, $p < .01$) and more unpleasant ($F = 4.28$, $p < .05$) than attractive children.

There was a three-way interaction, Severity $\times$ Attractiveness $\times$ Sex. Attractive males were rated more negatively for a severe offence than unattractive males ($F = 10.29$, $p < .01$) or attractive females ($F = 4.34$, $p < .05$).

DISCUSSION

Adults are influenced by perceived attractiveness when making judgements about a child's past and future behaviour, and about other aspects of the child's personality. They make attributional inferences on the basis of physical attractiveness, as predicted by the concept of the halo effect. Attractiveness also influences perceptions of the offence itself.

It seems reasonable to assume that these inferences lead to expectations which are communicated to the child, potentially influencing his/her self-evaluation and future conduct. Future research might find differences in the way attractive and unattractive children react to their own transgressions.

ISSUES TO THINK ABOUT

1 Dion made a point of justifying her sample. Why was this important?
2 Do you feel that the sample may have produced biased results? Why?
3 Attitudes were measured on a 17-centimetre line. What problems does a line of this length pose?
4 In the personality-trait dimensions, nine dimensions were included as fillers. Why?
5 Participants were given a lot of questions to answer. How might this have affected the results?
6 One set of questions identified participants who misunderstood the questions. How might you identify participants who were giving random answers because they didn't care?
7 Why were the participants randomly assigned to conditions?
8 List the controls used in this study, and comment on their effectiveness.
9 In the study each participant took part in only one condition, an independent participant's design. Would it be possible to use repeated measures? How? In what way would this be preferable?

10 Think of a real-life situation (such as a legal or medical one). Describe how you might apply the findings of this research.
11 This experiment involves deception of the participants. To what extent do you feel it is justified?
12 Why do you think that Chi-squared tests were used for some analyses and ANOVAs for others

REFERENCES

Dion, K.K. (1972) Physical attractiveness and evaluation of children's transgressions. *Journal of Personality and Social Psychology, 24(2)*, 207–13.

RECOMMENDED READING

Benson, P.L., Karabenick, S.A. and Lerner, R.M. (1976) Pretty pleases: The effects of physical attractiveness, race and sex on receiving help. *Journal of Experimental and Social Psychology, 12*, 409–15.

Dermer, M. and Thiel, D.L. (1975) When beauty may fail. *Journal of Personality and Social Psychology, 31*, 1168–76.

Dion, K., Bersheid, E. and Walster, E. (1972) What is beautiful is good. *Journal of Personality and Social Psychology, 24*, 285–90.

Harari, H. and McDavid, J.W. (1973) Teachers' expectations and name stereotypes. *Journal of Educational Psychology, 65*, 222–5.

Landy, D. and Sigall, H. (1974) Beauty is talent: Task evaluation as a function of the performer's physical attractiveness. *Journal of Personality and Social Psychology, 29*, 299–304.

OPTIMUM SEARCH STRATEGIES

Key terms: Impression formation, attractiveness, halo effect, popularity, development of self-concept, perception of wrongdoers/criminals.

Do-it-yourself: A Suggested Design

Hypothesis   Attractive children are perceived as being more honest than unattractive children.
[Optional: There is an association/interaction between attractiveness and severity of the transgression.]

Participants   Individuals over age 18.

Design   This is an independent measures experiment.

- Collect a set of photographs of children of about the same age. Use independent judges to determine attractiveness and select one 'attractive' and one 'unattractive' photograph.
- Write two stimulus paragraphs, both of which describe an impersonal transgression. One should be a mild transgression and the other a severe one, which could be confirmed by independent judges.
- Design an assessment tool. This should contain personality traits (including the target dimension honesty–dishonesty), and a means of assessing the perceived severity of the transgression (such as the undesirability of the act and/or the intensity of the punishment).
- Assign participants to one of the four experimental conditions (attractive/unattractive photograph and severe/mild transgression).
- Pilot study: It might be helpful to conduct a small study to test your design.

Ethical considerations
- Think carefully about the photographs you use and where they came from. You might not like your own photograph used in an experiment without your knowledge.
- Since this experiment calls for deception you should take special care with debriefing, providing *post-hoc* informed consent.
- You should avoid causing any unnecessary distress, respect confidentiality, and offer participants the right to withhold their data.

Controls
- Independent judges.
- Single blind.
- Filler questions to help disguise the experimental aim.
- Different experimental conditions.
- Randomised allocation to conditions.
- Standardised instructions and conditions.

Materials
- A set of photographs.
- Two stimulus paragraphs (as suggested in the key study) arranged for the four conditions.
- Assessment tools.
- Standardised instructions and debriefing document.

Analysis
- Descriptive statistics: means, clearly labelled tables of raw data, graphs.
- Unrelated test of difference: compare ratings for honesty in attractiveness/unattractiveness conditions regardless of the transgression.
- Optional hypothesis. Test of association: Chi-squared 2×2 for the mild transgression look at attractiveness (high/low) versus perceived undesirability (high/low). The same could be done for the severe transgression condition.
- Optional hypothesis. ANOVA 2×2 (between subjects): Attractiveness $\times$ Severity of Transgression.

practical
sixteen

DEFENSIVE ATTRIBUTION

OUTLINE

This experiment illustrates one particular kind of attributional bias, defensive attribution – the more serious an accident appears to be, the more people wish to assign responsibility to someone. Replication of this study calls for writing two descriptions – one of an accident and one of the person who may be responsible. These can be presented in written or oral form. Key ethical issues are deception and debriefing.

INTRODUCTION

Attribution theory describes how we make judgements about the causes of other people's behaviour and our own. We do so by making inferences about internal and external sources of causation. Such inferences or attributions might be based on past experience, but they are also often biased in a way that is self-serving. For example, when you fail an examination it is more comfortable to attribute the cause to your lecturer's poor teaching (an external attribution) than to your own lack of ability or effort (an internal cause).

There is a range of attribution biases. The most important one is called the fundamental attribution bias – people prefer to explain the behaviour of others in terms of internal sources rather than external sources. Other biases include the actor–observer difference, ingroup bias and defensive attribution. This last bias can be illustrated by the example of an accident; people seek to attribute blame rather than to accept that accidents sometimes happen because of no one particular cause. The attribution of blame makes us feel safer because it suggests that control is possible. Lerner (1980) called this a 'just-world-hypothesis'; our defensive response to disasters is a way of reducing our anxieties.

the key study

Walster (1966) investigated defensive attribution, specifically the conditions under which people seek to assign responsibility and whether the magnitude of an accident influences attributions of blame. The hypothesis was 'the worse the consequences of an accidental event, the greater the tendency for people to assign responsibility for the accident to someone possibly responsible for the accident'.

METHOD

Participants

Eighty-eight students on an introductory psychology course; both sexes were equally represented.

Design

There were four conditions:

1 Only the person responsible suffers; damage is inconsequential.
2 Only the person responsible suffers; damage is considerable.
3 Persons in addition to the potentially responsible person suffer; damage is inconsequential.
4 Persons in addition to the potentially responsible person suffer; damage is considerable.

Conditions 2 and 4 are the experimental conditions; conditions 1 and 3 are the respective control conditions. Conditions 1 and 2 test whether responsibility is assigned in relation to the severity of the consequences even when only the person responsible suffers, while conditions 3 and 4 test generally whether responsibility is assigned to a possibly responsible person when the consequences are serious.

The conditions were presented on four tapes representing conditions 1–4. On each tape there was:

A description of Lennie B by his mother, saying he was a good boy; he had a few neighbourhood problems when he was young but everything was fine now. A school teacher spoke, saying Lennie was a nice, enthusiastic person although he hadn't finished one of his school projects which might have been due to money problems at home. Then the accident was described. A neighbour stated in a casual, unemotional voice: 'that it was late this summer. Lennie had just bought a car – it was about six years old or so. He and his buddy drove up to Duluth and parked at the top of this hill. Lennie's buddy said Lennie did set the handbrake, but while they were gone the car started rolling. Some police who checked the car later said the brake cable was pretty badly rusted and must have broken. Anyway, the car started rolling . . .'

On Tape 1 this continued:

'If the car had run all the way down the hill, it would have crashed into a big tree that's at the bottom. But the car didn't go very far at all. . . . It rolled against an old stump that was sticking out a little way into the street and stopped. The car just got a tiny dent in the front bumper and that's all. Lennie didn't have any insurance at the time.'

On Tape 2 the last segment was:

'The car might have rolled to a stop against an old stump that was sticking out a little way into the street just in front of where the car was parked. Instead the car just missed it and went rolling all the way down the hill. . . . The car hit this really big tree that's at the bottom and then kind of bounced off it on to some others. The car was completely totalled; the impact bent the frame, rocked the engine off its mounts, bent the drive shaft – just completely ruined the front end. Lennie didn't have any insurance at the time.'

On Tape 3 the last segment was:

'If the car had run all the way down the hill, it would have crashed into this store that's right at the bottom, and probably hurt either a kid or the grocer who were in the store. But the car didn't go very far at all. . . .'

This continues as Tape 1.

On Tape 4 the last segment started as for Tape 2, and continued:

'Rolling all the way down the hill . . . the car really crashed through the window of this store that's right at the bottom. It hit a kid who was standing at the counter and the grocer. The kid was just dazed a little, but the grocer was hurt pretty badly. He was in hospital all last year. Lennie didn't have any insurance at the time.'

Note that tapes 1 and 2 differ only in terms of the actual consequences, while the possible consequences are the same. Tapes 3 and 4 differ from tapes 1 and 2 in terms of the possible consequences.

After hearing one of the four tapes, participants were asked the following questions:

1 Do you feel that any responsibility should be assigned to Lennie for the automobile accident in which (his fender was dented) (his car was demolished) (the child and the grocer were hurt)?

2 Lennie owned a car for five months before the accident occurred. Make as good a guess as you can whether or not he ever had his *brakes checked* during that period. (A 15-point scale was provided which ranged from 1 'I'm extremely sure he had a brake check' to 15 'I'm extremely sure he did *not* have a brake check'.)

3 Lennie's friend told their neighbour that Lennie set the *handbrake* before parking on the hill. How convinced are you that Lennie in fact did so? (Another 15-point scale was provided.)

4 Do you think that Lennie turned his wheels towards the curb before parking on the hill? (There were four alternative answers ranging from 1, 'He probably turned his wheels towards the curb *as far as possible*', to 4 , 'He probably did *not* turn his wheels towards the curb at all'.)

5 How often is a person 'morally responsible' for having his brakes and other safety devices checked? (The participant could fill in 'Every ——— months (years)' or tick 'A person is not *morally* responsible for having his brakes and safety devices checked'.) Answers to this question were awarded a mark between 1 and 6, where 6 was given for checks between every day and every two months.

6 There was finally a filler question about how much participants liked Lennie.

Procedure

Participants were tested in pairs. They were told that instead of serving as participants in the usual way they would have the chance to actually help select the materials and procedures for testing a hypothesis. They would listen to a tape and answer questions about the person described, which would help in selecting appropriate tapes. In this way, it was felt, participants would feel free to express their reactions.

Participants were assigned randomly to conditions and then given the appropriate tape and questions to listen to and complete on their own.

No mention is made of any debriefing in the journal article.

RESULTS

For Question 1 participants assigned greater responsibility when the consequences were serious (see Table 16.1).

More responsibility was assigned to Lennie by participants hearing Tape 2 than those hearing Tape 1 (*t*-test: $t = 2.2$, $p < .05$, two-tailed) and by more participants hearing Tape 4 than Tape 3 ($t = 2.0$, $p < .06$, two-tailed).

If we compare the mild outcomes (damage), we can see that the responsibility rating is almost the same regardless of whether only Lennie or others suffered. The same is true for the severe outcome. Significantly, more responsibility is assigned to Lennie for the severe accidents than the mild ones (using ANOVA, $F(1,84) = 8.73$, $p < .01$). This suggests that the most significant factor in Lennie's responsibility is whether the consequences are severe rather than who gets hurt.

However, there was a sex difference in this attribution. Women rated Lennie as equally responsible in conditions 3 and 4, whereas men made him more responsible in Condition 4. For women it apparently didn't matter whether the consequences were possible or actual; what was more significant was that others were involved.

Table 16.1 Mean responsibility assigned for the accident

Experimental condition	1	2	3	4
	Only Lennie suffers, damage is:		Others suffer, damage is:	
	Mild	*Severe*	*Mild*	*Severe*
Q1 Responsibility	2.5	3.0	2.6	3.2
Q2 Brakes	10.5	11.1	11.9	10.9
Q3 Handbrake	4.1	4.7	5.1	4.8
Q4 Turn wheels	3.5	3.7	3.5	3.6

The higher the mean the more responsible/careless Lennie was rated.
Source: Copyright © 1966 by the American Psychological Association. Reprinted with permission.

Questions 2, 3 and 4 together reflected the extent to which Lennie was judged as being 'careless'. A measure was calculated by adding together the three scores for the three questions after their variances had been equalised. An examination of the figures in Table 16.1 suggests that there was not a tendency to attribute greater carelessness to Lennie in conditions 2 and 4 than in 1 and 3, and this was supported by an analysis of variance ($F(1,84)=1.06$, *ns*). We can therefore conclude that Lennie's carelessness was judged more by the *possible* consequences than the *actual* consequences.

DISCUSSION

The hypothesis that greater responsibility is assigned when the consequences are greater has been supported, regardless of whether the consequences relate to the person responsible or to others. It also appears that people were harsher in their judgements of what precautions should have been taken when the consequences were more severe, again emphasising the role of the outcome in the attribution of blame. People don't look for someone to blame *unless* something serious happens; they then appear to have a greater need for a scapegoat.

A further study might look at whether a non-victim will be increasingly blamed for increasingly serious accidents.

The finding relating to sex differences might be considered in the light of Gilligan's view on moral reasoning and gender (see Practical 10, page 68).

ISSUES TO THINK ABOUT

1   Do you think it was important to use an equal number of males and females? Why?
2   To what extent do you feel that the questions enabled a valid assessment of Lennie's responsibility?
3   Why was a filler question included in the questionnaire? Was it necessary?
4   Do you think it was necessary to deceive the participants?
5   Should participants be debriefed? What should they be told and how might this affect the study as a whole?
6   In order to combine the results for questions 2, 3 and 4 the variances had to be equalised. Why is this necessary?
7   Walster did not plan to make any comparisons between conditions 1–2 and 3–4. In the light of the results, should she have done some statistical analysis on the means of these conditions? Why?
8   Walster reported that 'the brake check question was rewritten after the first 16 [participants] experienced difficulty answering it'. How could this have been avoided?
9   Does this study have any real-life applications?

REFERENCES

Lerner, M.J. (1980) *The belief in a just world: A fundamental delusion.* New York: Plenum.
Walster, E. (1966) The assignment of responsibility for an accident. *Journal of Personality and Social Psychology, 3,* 73–9.

RECOMMENDED READING

Jones, E.E., Rock, L., Shaver, K.G., Goethals, G.R. and Ward, L.M. (1968) Pattern of performance and ability to attribution: An unexpected primacy effect. *Journal of Personality and Social Psychology, 9,* 317–40.
Nisbett, R.E., Caputo, C., Legant, P. and Marecek, J. (1973) Behaviour as seen by the actor and as seen by the observer. *Journal of Personality and Social Psychology, 27,* 154–64.

OPTIMUM SEARCH STRATEGIES

Key terms: Attribution, defensive attribution, attribution bias, blame, responsibility.

Do-it-yourself: A Suggested Design

Hypothesis   More responsibility is assigned to individuals when the consequences of their action are more serious than when the consequences are less so.

Participants   Anyone.

Design   This is an independent measures experiment.

- Prepare two accounts of an accident that are similar in all respects except for the *actual* consequences. The accounts can be presented on paper or on tape.
- Prepare a questionnaire containing the question about the person's responsibility. There should be other filler questions.
- Randomly assign participants to conditions.

Ethical considerations
- Since this experiment involves deception you should take special care with debriefing, providing *post-hoc* informed consent.
- You should avoid causing any unnecessary distress, respect confidentiality, and offer participants the right to withhold their data.

Controls
- Experimental and control conditions.
- Randomised allocation to condition.
- Filler questions to prevent demand characteristics.
- Single blind.
- Standardised instructions and conditions.

Materials
- Stimulus tapes/paragraphs describing the accident.
- Questionnaire to assess responsibility.
- Standardised instructions and debriefing notes.

Analysis
- Descriptive statistics: means, clearly labelled tables and graphs.
- Unrelated test of difference: compare responsibility scores given by participants in both conditions.
- Optional: look at male/female differences using ANOVA to compare means between sexes and between conditions.

practical seventeen

ATTITUDES AND CLASSICAL CONDITIONING

OUTLINE

Attitudes are often learned through direct experience. This experiment demonstrates how attitudes can be classically conditioned by means of verbal communication. Replication calls for constructing stimulus word lists and consideration of several key ethical issues, namely the use of deception and the creation of negative attitudes.

INTRODUCTION

Attitudes have three components: affective (liking/disliking), cognitive (beliefs about a thing or person) and behaviour (a predisposition to behave towards the object in a particular manner).

An attitude may be acquired in a number of different ways. For example, there is evidence for some innate attitudes such as fear of spiders (Öhman *et al.*, 1975). Positive attitudes may develop through familiarity (Zajonc, 1968), and both positive and negative attitudes may result through social modelling and operant or classical conditioning.

the key study

Staats and Staats (1958) examined the classical conditioning of attitudes, testing the hypothesis that 'attitudes already elicited by socially significant verbal stimuli can be changed through classical conditioning, using other words as unconditioned stimuli'. The socially significant verbal stimuli would be national names and familiar masculine names. The 'other' words would be common nouns which had positive or negative connotations. The result would be a positive or negative attitude towards the socially significant stimuli.

METHOD

Participants

Ninety-three elementary psychology students as a fulfilment of their course requirement. The sex ratio was not stated.

Design

Experiment I

- The conditioned stimulus (CS): CS words were national names. The six names used were: *German*, *Swedish*, *Italian*, *French*, *Dutch* and *Greek*. They were presented by slide projection at five-second intervals.
- The unconditioned stimulus (US): US words were presented orally by the experimenter approximately one second after the CS word.
- Each CS word was presented 18 times; thus 108 different US words were used.

The participants were divided into two equal groups.

- For Group 1 the word *Dutch* was paired with words that had a positive evaluative meaning, such as *gift*, *sacred*, *happy*. The word *Swedish* was paired with words which had a negative evaluative meaning, such as *bitter*, *ugly*, *failure*.
- For Group 2 this was reversed.
- All other CS words were paired with neutral words such as *chair*, *with*, *twelve*.

See page 122 for full stimulus list.

Experiment II

- The CS names were: *Harry*, *Tom*, *Jim*, *Ralph*, *Bill* and *Bob*. Tom and Bill were the target words.

Assessment

Attitudes towards visually presented words were assessed at the end on a 7-point semantic differential scale from pleasant to unpleasant.

Procedure

The participants were first given a training task to prepare them for the actual experimental phase. In the first task they had to learn five visually presented national names, each shown four times, in random order. The second task was to learn 33 auditorily presented words. The participant had to repeat each word after the experimenter. They were tested by being given 12 word pairs and having to recognise which of each pair had just been presented.

They were then told that the purpose of the experiment was to study 'how both these kinds of learning take place together – the effect that one has upon the other, and so on'. They were told to learn the visually presented words by looking at them and to simultaneously concentrate on saying the auditorily presented words.

When this conditioning phase was completed, participants were shown each of the target CS words and asked to indicate their attitudes and whether the word had been on the list.

They were then tested on the auditorily presented words and finally asked to write anything that came to mind about the experiment, such as what they might have thought was its purpose, since this might have affected their performance.

RESULTS

Seventeen participants indicated that they were aware of a systematic CS–US relationship; therefore their data were excluded from the analysis. This meant that an additional four participants had to be excluded in order to maintain the balance in conditions. This resulted in a final total of 24 participants in Experiment I and 48 in Experiment II.

In both experiments, a 'negative evaluative variable' (i.e. a negative US paired with the CS) led to a significantly more unpleasant attitude (7 = unpleasant). Table

Table 17.1 Means and SDs of conditioned attitude scores

		Names			
		Dutch		Swedish	
	Group	Mean	SD	Mean	SD
Experiment I	1	2.67	0.94	3.42	1.50
	2	2.67	1.31	1.83	0.90

		Tom		Bill	
		Mean	SD	Mean	SD
Experiment II	1	2.71	2.01	4.12	2.04
	2	3.42	2.55	1.79	1.07

Note: Pleasant was scored as 1, unpleasant as 7.

Table 17.2 Summary of the results of the analysis of variance for each experiment

Source		Experiment I			Experiment II		
		df	MS	F	df	MS	F
Between Ss	Groups	1	7.52	4.36*	1	15.84	5.00*
	Error	22	1.73		46	3.17	
Within	Conditioned attitude	1	7.52	5.52*	1	55.51	10.47**
	Names	1	0.02	0.01	1	0.26	0.05
	Residual	22	1.36		46	5.30	
Total		47			95		

* $= p < .05$
** $= p < .01$

17.1 shows that in all cases but the Dutch CS, being paired with a negative US word led to a less pleasant attitude towards the CS word. Table 17.2 shows that conditioning occurred in both experiments.

DISCUSSION

The experiment demonstrated that participants' attitudinal responses could be changed through verbal communications, as distinct from direct experience. This can explain how certain comments, such as 'the Dutch are honest' will lead people to form positive attitudes towards such nationals.

There is no evidence of behaviour change towards individuals but only towards the labels themselves.

ISSUES TO THINK ABOUT

1 In what way might the sample used have biased the results?
2 Why were the US words said one second after the CS words were shown?
3 How were attitudes assessed? Draw your own representation of the assessment 'tool' for attitudes.
4 In what way do you think the 'training task' was an important part of the experiment?
5 How do you think the exclusion of 17 participants may have affected the results?
6 Can you suggest why the response to the Dutch CS word was different from the others?

7 Do you feel that the deception involved was justified? How might any objections be overcome?
8 A further ethical issue was the conditioning of attitudes, especially negative ones. Do you feel this is unacceptable? How might the experimenters have made it more acceptable?
9 How might these results be usefully applied?

REFERENCES

Öhman, A., Erixson, G. and Lofberg, L. (1975) Phobias and preparedness: Phobic and neutral pictures as conditioned stimuli for human autonomic responses. *Journal of Abnormal Psychology, 84*, 41–5.

Staats, A.W. and Staats, C.K. (1958) Attitudes established by classical conditioning. *Journal of Abnormal and Social Psychology, 57*, 37–40.

Zajonc, R.B. (1968) Attitudinal effects of mere exposure. *Journal of Personality and Social Psychology (Monograph), 9*, 1–29.

RECOMMENDED READING

Harari, H. and McDavid, J.W. (1973) Teachers' expectations and name stereotypes. *Journal of Educational Psychology, 65*, 222–5.

Karlins, M., Coffman, T.L. and Walters, G. (1969) On the fading of social stereotypes: Studies in three generations of college students. *Journal of Personality and Social Psychology, 13*, 1–16.

Katz, D. and Braly, K. (1933) Racial stereotypes of one hundred college students. *Journal of Abnormal and Social Psychology, 28*, 280–90.

OPTIMUM SEARCH STRATEGIES

Key terms: Attitudes, attitude formation, classical conditioning, prejudice, nationalism, stereotypes.

Do-it-yourself: A Suggested Design

Hypothesis	Words paired with negative unconditioned stimuli (US) are rated as more unpleasant than words paired with positive US.
Participants	Anyone, but preferably not children because of the ethical considerations.
Design	This is an independent and related measures experiment.

- Decide on six words as conditioned stimuli (CS), for example, unusual last names. There are important ethical considerations about forming negative attitudes and therefore you should select your US carefully. You must consider the attitudes you may create.
- Compile a list of 108 US; 18 of these should have a positive evaluative meaning, and 18 should have a negative meaning. You can use the words chosen by Staats and Staats (see page 122). Their connotations can be checked with independent judges.
- For one group of participants the target word should be paired with positive US and the second word should be paired with negative US. For the other group of participants this should be reversed (for example, for Group 1 Jones is paired with negative words and Smith is paired with positive words. The reverse is done for Group 2). Visually displayed words can be shown on cards, and auditorily presented words can be spoken by the experimenter.
- Prepare the order of presentation to avoid any order effects.
- Devise an answer sheet to include a semantic differential to rate the six CS.

Ethical considerations
- You should remember informed consent, deception, distress and confidentiality. You must debrief participants, offering them the right to withhold their data.
- You must carefully consider the US selected for this experiment. It is particularly important that participants should be in the same state before and after the experiment, that is they should have the same attitudes.

Controls
- Negative and positive US words balanced for frequency.
- Random order of CS words.
- Independent judges to confirm positive and negative US words.
- Single blind.
- Different experimental conditions.
- Randomised allocation to conditions.
- Standardised instructions and conditions.

Materials
- Word lists and answer sheets.
- Standardised instructions and debriefing notes.

Analysis
- Descriptive statistics: mean, clearly labelled tables and graphs.
- Compare means:
  - ANOVA 2×2 (between and within subjects) Group $\times$ Names.
  - *Or* test of related difference, comparing the score for all participants on the negatively labelled CS and on the positively labelled CS.

List of CS–US word pairs

DUTCH – beauty	SWEDISH – worthless	SWEDISH – sick	GERMAN – note
FRENCH – with	SWEDISH – sour	FRENCH – ship	GERMAN – stick
SWEDISH – thief	GREEK – the	FRENCH – room	DUTCH – success
FRENCH – car	SWEDISH – enemy	SWEDISH – stupid	GREEK – sock
DUTCH – win	GREEK – box	FRENCH – deck	GREEK – six
GERMAN – pen	GREEK – clay	FRENCH – mop	FRENCH – the
ITALIAN – key	FRENCH – this	ITALIAN – glass	ITALIAN – side
GREEK – chair	SWEDISH – cruel	GERMAN – into	FRENCH – light
FRENCH – paper	GREEK – sand	SWEDISH – failure	FRENCH – three
FRENCH – cord	SWEDISH – dirty	ITALIAN – shoe	GREEK – saucer
DUTCH – gift	DUTCH – sacred	SWEDISH – disgusting	DUTCH – money
SWEDISH – bitter	DUTCH – friend	DUTCH – happy	ITALIAN – quilt
ITALIAN – book	FRENCH – leaf	DUTCH – pretty	FRENCH – it
FRENCH – letter	SWEDISH – evil	GERMAN – glove	ITALIAN – truck
DUTCH – sweet	GERMAN – string	SWEDISH – agony	FRENCH – ground
FRENCH – in	GREEK – and	ITALIAN – cart	GERMAN – water
DUTCH – honest	GREEK – dot	GREEK – wheel	ITALIAN – garage
ITALIAN – radio	GERMAN – line	GERMAN – on	SWEDISH – poison
SWEDISH – ugly	GERMAN – train	GERMAN – sofa	GREEK – twelve
GERMAN – four	DUTCH – valuable	GREEK – dresser	ITALIAN – ink
ITALIAN – cup	FRENCH – table	GERMAN – trunk	ITALIAN – store
SWEDISH – sad	GERMAN – can	SWEDISH – fear	GREEK – number
GERMAN – five	ITALIAN – word	GERMAN – those	ITALIAN – hat
DUTCH – smart	ITALIAN – pencil	SWEDISH – insane	ITALIAN – eleven
GREEK – up	DUTCH – steak	GREEK – fork	GERMAN – shirt
GERMAN – pot	GREEK – clock	GREEK – eight	DUTCH – vacation
DUTCH – rich	ITALIAN – of	DUTCH – healthy	DUTCH – love

Source: Staats and Staats (1958)

practical *eighteen*

PRODUCT PERSONALITIES

OUTLINE

This study provides evidence that people hold consistent stereotypes about the owners of cars. Stereotypes were elicited using an adjective check list. Such stereotypes are important in product marketing. Replication involves constructing your own check list and testing attitudes. A key issue is how the study could be better designed with statistics in mind.

INTRODUCTION

The aim of advertising is to promote a particular product in a way that will increase sales. An integral part of any product is its image and its association with a certain group of users. For example, some beer companies promote the idea that dynamic, attractive, young people are the kind of people who drink their product; therefore one way to acquire that image is to be seen drinking the product.

The associations related to products are particularly important when there are a number of physically similar products, such as beers or cigarettes. Companies must then try to distinguish themselves by creating a special image. One way to study these associations is to look at the stereotypes people hold about various products.

the key study

Wells et al. *(1957) used an adjective check list to elicit a set of car stereotypes because they believed it was the simplest and easiest method. They were not testing any prediction as such but investigating the use of the adjective check list as a means of eliciting stereotypes.*

METHOD

Participants

One hundred students (no more details are given).

Design

The adjectives in Table 18.1 were taken from the Thorndike–Lorge (1944) word list (more are shown in Appendix I). The ones selected were those that the authors felt would be the best-known. They excluded words such as 'handsome' and 'clear', which did not apply to car owners.

Table 18.1 Selected adjectives from the Thorndike–Lorge word list

friendly	strong	angry	popular	fat
slow	good	married	strange	patient
modern	secure	vain	fair	tender
comfortable	particular	merry	small	honest
poor	natural	sharp	serious	gay
masculine	sad	different	big	silent
gentle	young	set	cold	superior
firm	average	clean	rough	simple
travelled	dangerous	wise	hard	content
understanding	old-fashioned	successful	cheap	soft
middle class	able	warm	democratic	thin
good-looking	common	quiet	fancy	old
feminine	practical	moral	cross	kind
difficult	thinking	powerful	careful	low class
tired	important	foreign	interesting	little
brave	rich	plain	bright	weak
loud	busy	nice	original	happy
heavy	smart	active	correct	calm
curious	proud	bitter	cool	single
pleasant	bad	steady	famous	religious
funny	wonderful	fine	independent	smooth
ordinary	tall	high class		

Wells *et al.* argued that, if participants were just asked to tick the adjectives which describe a particular car, they would be reluctant to make discriminations unless they felt quite confident. An alternative system would be to ask participants to tick the kind of person each adjective describes best (for example, a Cadillac owner, a Buick owner and a Chevrolet owner). This would force the participant to make a discrimination, though it has the disadvantage of making judgements relative rather than absolute.

To avoid 'systematic fatigue effects' the total list was divided into five sub-lists which were rotated, and the car names were also rotated to balance any tendency to tick the first, middle or last column.

Procedure

Participants were asked to indicate which car owner the adjective best describes. They were asked first to complete the adjective list for Cadillac, Buick and Chevrolet owners, then Chevrolet, Ford and Plymouth owners.

RESULTS

Table 18.2 shows the traits most often associated with each car; only those traits whose frequencies exceed chance expectations at the .01 level or beyond are shown.

Table 18.2 Car owners and their most consistent traits

Car owner	Stereotype
Cadillac	rich, high class, famous, important, fancy, proud, superior, successful, cold, vain, particular, big, fat, powerful
Buick	middle class, brave, masculine, strong, modern, pleasant
Chevrolet	poor, low class, ordinary, plain, simple, practical, common, average, cheap, thin, little, friendly, small
Ford	masculine, young, powerful, good-looking, rough, dangerous, strong, single, merry, loud, active, cool, tall, interesting, sharp, popular
Plymouth	quiet, careful, slow, silent, moral, fat, gentle, calm, sad, thinking, patient, honest, understanding, content

Note: trait names are listed by frequency of mention.

DISCUSSION

The study shows that stereotypes associated with the owners of well-known automobiles can be elicited using an adjective check list.

ISSUES TO THINK ABOUT

1 Participants had to place a tick next to each adjective for each set of three cars. How do you think this affected the overall responses?
2 Do you feel that an adjective check list is a valid means of eliciting stereotypes? Explain your answer.
3 How else could stereotypes be elicited?
4 Wells *et al.* say, 'it is obvious that results obtained from 100 college students can *not* be thought of as characteristic of the consumer population. However, the changes that occurred within this limited population provide a 'test tube' demonstration.' Do you think this assumption is reasonable?
5 What are 'systematic fatigue effects'? How might they have influenced the results in this study?
6 How might one design this study so that an inferential statistical test could be used?
7 What descriptive statistics would enhance the reader's understanding?
8 Is it ethical to study stereotypes? Consider other studies, such as Katz and Braly (1933).
9 Do you think that such stereotyping would have changed since 1957?

REFERENCES

Katz, D. and Braly, K. (1933) Racial stereotypes of one hundred college students. *Journal of Abnormal and Social Psychology, 28*, 280–90.

Thorndike, E.L. and Lorge, I. (1944) *The teacher's word book of 30,000 words.* New York: Teacher's College, Columbia University.

Wells, W.D., Andriuli, F.J., Goi, F.J. and Seader, S.A. (1957) An adjective checklist for the study of 'product personality'. *Journal of Applied Psychology, 41*, 317–19.

RECOMMENDED READING

Heckler, H.E. and Childers, T.L. (1992) The role of expectancy and relevancy in memory for verbal and visual information: What is incongruency? *Journal of Consumer Research, 18,* 475–92.

Staats, A.W. and Staats, C.K. (1958) Attitudes established by classical conditioning. *Journal of Abnormal and Social Psychology, 57,* 37–40. [And see Practical 17, page 116.]

Yalch, R.F. (1991) Memory in a jingle jungle: Music as a mnemonic device in communicating advertising slogans. *Journal of Applied Psychology, 76,* 268–75.

OPTIMUM SEARCH STRATEGIES

Key terms: Stereotypes, product personality, cars, advertising, attitudes.

Do-it-yourself: A Suggested Design

Hypothesis   Owners of different cars are perceived as possessing consistently different personality traits.
Participants   Anyone.
Design   This is a survey of attitudes.

- Compile a list of commonly known and relevant adjectives (word lists are provided in Appendix I). You might ask an independent judge to sort these into a positive group and a negative group. You might also take Wells *et al.*'s findings into consideration.
- Compile different versions of adjective lists to prevent order effects.
- Randomise allocation of lists to participants.
- Select the names of several common cars. Ask participants to tick one car for each adjective (forced choice).

Ethical considerations
- Since this experiment involves deception, you should take special care with debriefing, providing *post-hoc* informed consent.
- You should avoid causing any unnecessary distress, respect confidentiality and offer participants the right to withhold their data.

Controls
- Presentation order varied.
- Different experimental conditions.
- Random allocation of lists to participants.
- Single blind.
- Standardised instructions and conditions.

Materials
- Adjective lists.
- Answer sheets, listing kinds of cars.
- Standardised instructions and debriefing notes.

Analysis
- Descriptive statistics: means, clearly labelled tables and graphs.
- Compare frequencies for key adjectives, such as rich or careful (you can decide which are 'key adjectives' when designing the study, or *post-hoc*, when you see which adjectives were selected most often). For each car, record frequencies for these adjectives. Use a Chi-squared test.
- Group positive and negative adjectives. For each car record frequencies for these adjectives. Use a Chi-squared test.

practical nineteen

ESP: A 'SHEEP–GOAT EFFECT'

OUTLINE

This experiment demonstrates that people who believe in para-normal phenomena (called 'sheep') are less good at tasks involving subjective probability than people who do not ('goats'). Subjective probability can be defined as one's intuitive sense of how likely something is. Replication involves easy data collection.

INTRODUCTION

Parapsychologists explain extrasensory perception and psychokinesis in terms of 'psi', a hypothetical force not related to any known sensory system. There are alternative explanations for these so-called psi phenomena.

For example, Schmeidler and McConnell (1958) distinguished between 'sheep' and 'goats', respectively believers and nonbelievers in psi phenomena. They found that sheep consistently scored higher on psi tasks than did goats, and they called this a 'sheep–goat effect'. This effect suggests that belief in the paranormal positively or negatively influences performance, depending on whether you are a sheep or goat. However, we cannot be certain whether a person's initial belief is a cause of psi performance or an effect.

A second explanation was put forward by Blackmore (1992). She suggested that psi phenomena are cognitive illusions. In the same way that visual illusions tell us about our perceptual systems, psi 'illusions' tell us about the way we think. People like to be able to explain things that happen around them, but some events have no cause; they simply coincide with other events as a consequence of chance. For example, you might be thinking of someone and at that very moment that person happens to telephone you. Some people would say 'we must be telepathic', others would say 'now, that's a coincidence'. Psychic events create the expectation of an explanation when in fact there is none – they create an illusion of causality. Sheep prefer the explanation of psi, goats accept the explanation of randomness.

the key study

Brugger et al. *(1990) used subjective random generation (SRG) to measure perception of randomness. In an SRG task a person is asked to generate a set of random occurrences, such as a string of numbers. A truly random string would have many instances of repetition. However, when people are generating a random sequence they tend to avoid these repetitions; this is termed 'repetition avoidance'. The same bias can be seen in the 'gambler's fallacy' – the roulette player's mistaken assumption that the probability that a red number will appear increases after a run of black numbers, whereas the probabilities do not change. This illustrates subjective probability, as distinct from mathematically calculated probability.*

It is possible that repetition avoidance may explain why some people appear to do well on tasks of ESP. When both participants are generating similar pseudo-random sequences they are more likely to coincide in their responses than when one or both of them are generating true random sequences.

The research question in this experiment was 'whether or not sheep and goats differ in their subjective randomness, as measured by the individual avoidance of repetitions'.

METHOD EXPERIMENT 1: EXTRASENSORY PERCEPTION

Participants

Sixty-two undergraduate psychology students, tested in groups of four to six. There were 19 males and 43 females.

Design

Zener cards were used. These have one of five symbols on them: a circle, cross, star, square or wavy lines. The order of exposure was determined with a computer-generated random-number sequence.

Participants' responses were recorded on a form organised in rows, where each row contained all five possible symbols. Scoring was done by looking at the direction of the choice from one trial to the next, because responses were considered as being 'a vertically arranged sequence of spatial directional decisions'. A mark placed in the same column or one placed to the left or right after a previous decision in the same direction was considered as a repetition. The total number of repetitions of directional choices was recorded.

Procedure

The experimenter (E1) looked at a card. In another, darkened room a second experimenter (E2) sat with the participant (P), and when a communication light came on, said that E1 was 'sending'. P then circled the symbol on the answer sheet that they 'received'.

This was repeated 10 times, and then P was asked to rate his/her belief in the paranormal on a 6-point scale.

METHOD   EXPERIMENT 2: SUBJECTIVE RANDOM GENERATION

Participants

Forty-eight medical and biology students were tested individually (24 men and 24 women aged between 20 and 40).

Design

Participants had to mimic the rolling of a die. They were asked to say the digits from 1 to 6 so as 'to make the resulting sequence as indistinguishable as possible from that of an actually rolled die'. Their responses were paced at one response per second with a metronome.

The score on this task was equivalent to the number of consecutive repetitions of the same digit.

Procedure

Participants repeated the task 66 times, that is, 66 responses. Afterwards they were asked to indicate their belief in the paranormal on a 6-point scale.

METHOD   EXPERIMENT 3: APPRECIATION OF RANDOMNESS

Participants

As for Experiment 2.

Design

Each participant was shown two strings of six numbers, each string being described as the outcome of a die being thrown. One of the strings contained more repetitions than the other.

Procedure

Participants were asked to imagine a situation where they had to wait for one of the two strings to occur. They were asked to say which was more likely to appear first:

- (1) String 1.
- (2) Both equally likely.
- (3) String 2.

This was repeated six times. The correct choice each time was String 2, since any two strings are equally likely to appear.

RESULTS

In Experiment 1 three participants were discarded because they did not complete their response sheets properly. The remaining participants could be divided into 28 sheep (those who indicated a 1 or 2 on the belief scale), 17 goats (5 or 6 on the scale) or indifferent (3 or 4). Brugger *et al.* found that sheep showed fewer directional responses than goats (see Figure 19.1(a)).

Figures 19.1 (b) and 19.1 (c) show that the results for the other two experiments followed the same pattern. In Experiment 2, sheep showed significantly fewer repetitions than goats ($t = 1.8$, $p < .05$). In Experiment 3 sheep answered significantly less correctly ($t = 2.8$, $p < .005$).

In all three experiments all the participants performed below the levels of chance. For example, in Experiment 1 the chance level was 4.5, whereas the mean for all participants was 3.0 (Wilcoxon $z = 5.58$, $p < .001$). In Experiment 2, 10.8 was the expected number of consecutive repetitions; the mean was 5.9 for all participants (Wilcoxon $z = 5.7$, $p < .001$). This suggests some subjective-probability bias for all participants – sheep and goats.

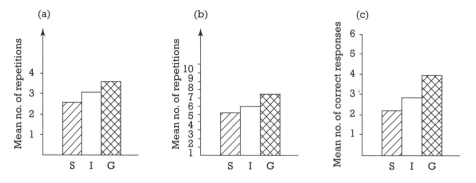

Figure 19.1 Mean number of repetitive targets for sheep (S), indifferent participants (I) and goats (G) in (a) ESP task (Experiment 1), (b) SRG task (Experiment 2) and (c) randomness appreciation task (Experiment 3)
Source: Reprinted with permission from Brugger *et al.* (1990). Copyright © The British Psychological Society.

DISCUSSION

It is clear that everyone has a tendency to be biased against repetitions. This experiment also demonstrates that people who believe in psi phenomena (sheep) are more biased than nonbelievers (goats), thus confirming the notion of sheep–goat effects. This could therefore explain experiences of psi phenomena, although it could be that sheep really do experience more coincidences in life, and therefore that their bias against randomness is a reflection of their reality rather than their tendency to think in a certain way. However, in Experiment 3 all participants were given the opportunity to respond to 'reality' and sheep demonstrated a clear resistance to recognising the facts of probability.

Brugger *et al.* end by suggesting that ESP stands for an *E*ffect of *S*ubjective *P*robability.

ISSUES TO THINK ABOUT

1 There is no statement about whether participants were volunteers or not. Do you think it is important to state your sampling method? Why might it be important?

2 In Experiment 1, why was it important to use a random-number sequence to generate the order of the Zener cards?

3 In Experiment 1, Brugger *et al.* assessed SRG on the basis of direction of response. Do you think this was a valid way to measure the dependent variable?

4 In Experiment 1 there were 10 trials, whereas in Experiment 2 there were 66 trials. Which is preferable? Why?

5 A 'Belief in the Paranormal Scale' is included on page 136. In Brugger *et al.*'s experiment they simply asked participants to rate their belief on a 6-point scale. Suggest the relative advantages/disadvantages of each method.

6 Is it important that belief is assessed after the SRG task? Why?

7 In Experiment 2 a metronome paced the responses. Why might this be important?

8 The same students participated in Experiments 2 and 3. Would it matter if some did Experiment 2 and then 3, and others did 3 and then 2? Why?

9 In Experiment 1 some of the participants were 'discarded'. In what way might this affect the results?

10 Why was the *t*-test chosen to analyse the results of Experiments 2 and 3?

REFERENCES

Blackmore, S.J. (1992) Psychic experiences: Psychic illusions. *Skeptical Inquirer, 16,* 367–76.

Brugger, P., Landis, T. and Regard, M. (1990) A 'sheep–goat effect' in repetition avoidance: Extra-sensory perception as an effect of subjective probability. *British Journal of Psychology, 81,* 455–68.

Schmeidler, G.R. and McConnell, R.A. (1958) *ESP and personality patterns.* New Haven, CT: Yale University Press.

RECOMMENDED READING

Blackmore, S. and Troscianko, T. (1985) Belief in the paranormal: Probability judgements, illusory control, and the 'chance baseline shift'. *British Journal of Psychology, 76,* 459–68.

Langer, E.J. and Roth, J. (1975) Heads I win, tails it's chance: The illusion of control as a function of the sequence of outcomes in a purely chance task. *Journal of Personality and Social Psychology, 32,* 951–5.

OPTIMUM SEARCH STRATEGIES

Key terms: SRG, randomness, gambler's fallacy, cognitive illusions, psi phenomena, sheep and goats, paranormal.

Do-it-yourself: A Suggested Design

Hypothesis   Sheep produce fewer repetitions in an SRG task than goats.
Participants   Anyone.
Design   This is an independent measures natural experiment.

- Ask participants to 'mimic' the rolling of a die, as suggested above.
- How many trials are necessary? Enough to find a difference between sheep and goats. If you had only 10 trials, it would be hard to detect any difference. A pilot study might be useful.
- Assess paranormal attitudes on a simple scale, as above, or the 'Belief in the Paranormal Scale' on page 136. This should be done after the die task to avoid demand characteristics.

Ethical considerations
- Since this experiment involves deception, you should take special care with debriefing, providing *post-hoc* informed consent.
- You should avoid causing any unnecessary distress, respect confidentiality and offer participants the right to withhold their data.

Controls
- Validated questionnaire or a means of assessing paranormal belief.
- Single blind.
- Standardised instructions and conditions.

Materials
- Paper to record participants' answers.
- Metronome to time response rate.
- Standardised instructions and debriefing notes.

Analysis
- Descriptive statistics: means, clearly labelled tables and graphs; look at the performance of sheep, goats and indifferent participants.
- Unrelated test of difference. Compare performance of sheep and goats on die-rolling task.
- Optional: ANOVA 1×3. Compare performance of sheep, goats and indifferent participants.

BELIEF IN THE PARANORMAL SCALE

Instructions

This inventory represents an attempt to discover which of the various paranormal events and phenomena you believe to be most likely and which you believe to be least likely. There are no right or wrong answers. Moreover, this is not an attempt to belittle or make fun of your own beliefs. Therefore please indicate your true feelings as well as you can. If you are unsure or ambivalent so indicate by marking 'undecided' and proceed to the next item. Indicate your answers in the following format:

1 = strongly disagree with statement
2 = disagree with statement
3 = undecided or don't know
4 = agree with statement
5 = strongly agree with statement

1 2 3 4 5	1.	I believe psychic phenomena are real, and should become a part of psychology and be studied scientifically.
1 2 3 4 5	2.	All UFO sightings are either other forms of physical phenomena (such as weather balloons) or simply hallucinations.
1 2 3 4 5	3.	I am convinced the Abominable Snowman of Tibet really exists.
1 2 3 4 5	4.	I firmly believe that ghosts and spirits do exist.
1 2 3 4 5	5.	Black magic really exists and should be dealt with in a serious manner.
1 2 3 4 5	6.	Witches and warlocks do exist.
1 2 3 4 5	7.	Only the uneducated or demented believe in the supernatural and the occult.
1 2 3 4 5	8.	Through psychic individuals it is possible to communicate with the dead.
1 2 3 4 5	9.	I believe the Loch Ness monster of Scotland exists.
1 2 3 4 5	10.	I believe that once a person dies his spirit may come back from time to time in the form of ghosts.
1 2 3 4 5	11.	Some individuals are able to levitate (lift objects) through mysterious mental forces.

continued

1 2 3 4 5 12.	I believe that many special persons throughout the world have the ability to predict the future.
1 2 3 4 5 13.	The idea of being able to tell the future through the means of palm reading represents the beliefs of foolish and unreliable persons.
1 2 3 4 5 14.	I am firmly convinced that reincarnation has been occurring throughout history and that it will continue to occur.
1 2 3 4 5 15.	I firmly believe that, at least on some occasions, I can read another person's mind via ESP (extrasensory perception).
1 2 3 4 5 16.	ESP is an unusual gift that many persons have and should not be confused with elaborate tricks used by entertainers.
1 2 3 4 5 17.	Ghosts and witches do not exist outside the realm of the imagination.
1 2 3 4 5 18.	Supernatural phenomena should become part of scientific study, equal in importance to physical phenomena.
1 2 3 4 5 19.	All the reports of 'scientific proof' of psychic phenomena are strictly sensationalism with no factual basis.
1 2 3 4 5 20.	Through the use of mysterious formulas and incantations it is possible to cast spells on individuals.
1 2 3 4 5 21.	With proper training anyone could learn to read other people's minds.
1 2 3 4 5 22.	It is advisable to consult your horoscope daily.
1 2 3 4 5 23.	Plants can sense the feelings of people through a form of ESP.
1 2 3 4 5 24.	ESP has been scientifically proven to exist.
1 2 3 4 5 25.	There is a great deal we have yet to understand about the mind of man, so it is likely that many phenomena (such as ESP) will one day be proven to exist.

Scoring

Reverse responses for questions 2, 7, 13, 17, 19. Add all responses, giving a maximum of 125.

The original scale had 77 items, which were tested on 92 undergraduates. With the aid of a Likert analysis those items easiest to discriminate were selected while maintaining a balance in content categories. The categories represented are: supernatural, occult, divination and prediction, psychic phenomena, physical manifestations, creatures and civilisations, and general.

The revised 25-item version was standardised on 475 undergraduates (279 female, 196 male):

Mean score = 69.09, standard deviation = 13.38
Persons who scored less than 50 = 10% (low believers)
Persons who scored more than 85 = 10% (high believers)

Source: Jones, W.H., Russell, D.W. and Nickel T.W. (1977) Belief in the Paranormal Scale: an instrument to measure beliefs in magical phenomena and causes. *JSAS Catalogue of Selected Documents in Psychology*, *7:100* (Ms. no. 1577).

practical twenty

THE RESPONSE OF BLACK BEARS TO HUMAN COMPANY

> **OUTLINE**
>
> In this study four black bears in two zoos were observed with the intention of determining whether the presence of human observers was related to systematic changes in the bears' behaviour. An ethogram (grid of behaviours) was used to assist in organising systematic observations of behaviour. Key methodological and ethical issues are raised regarding the naturalistic observation of animals.

INTRODUCTION

All research aims to be valid. One measure of this is ecological validity – the extent to which the behaviour being researched is similar to its naturally occurring version. When animal behaviour is observed, even in natural surroundings, there is the possibility that the mere presence of an observer may affect the target behaviour, therefore challenging the validity of the research.

This is a kind of experimenter or researcher effect, and an example of participant reactivity. An experimenter effect is some aspect of the experiment that has an effect on the participants in the research. 'Participant reactivity' is a concept that represents the extent to which any research participant, human or non-human animal, is an active part of the research process and not a passive subject that might react like a substance in a chemical experiment. Even this latter conception may be a false belief; Heisenberg's uncertainty principle states that we cannot observe something without changing it. He pointed out that you cannot determine both the position and the velocity of a subatomic particle simultaneously because when you undertake to measure one, you change the other measurement.

the key study

Jordan and Burghardt (1986) suggested that the methodological problem of participant reactivity 'may reach its acme of potential for confounding research in observational studies of complex behavioural repertoires'. Participant reactivity of non-human animals may challenge the validity of data collected in naturalistic studies, and may also raise ethical questions in terms of the adverse effects that even unobtrusive observers may have on the animals.

Studies have been made of the reactivity of humans to observers, indicating that their behaviour is systematically changed. Previous studies of bears suggest that only erratic movements of observers draw attention and that the bears soon get used to the presence of observers. However, such studies focus on 'between-sessions' comparisons rather than 'within-sessions'. This study therefore aimed to analyse how rates of various behaviour patterns changed within and between observation sessions of bears with respect to the presence of the observers.

METHOD

Participants

The researchers studied a total of 20 black bears over a three-year period, but in this report focused on four bears caught in the wild and reared by humans from the time of capture.

One male–female pair (A and B) lived in a 17- by 88-metre enclosure at Goldrush Junction (now Dollywood). The bears of the other pair were both females (C and D) living at the Tremont Environmental Education Centre in an 18- by 18-metre enclosure. Plans of both enclosures are shown in Figure 20.1

Design

Observations were recorded at 30-second intervals, at which time an instantaneous scan sample or record was made with an ethogram developed for the study. The ethogram was divided into four classes:

- Class P: Postures and locomotions (see Table 20.1).
- Class S: Sounds, such as panting, moaning and huffing followed by jaw-popping, snorting and slapping, followed immediately by panting.
- Class F: Functional activities, consisting of such categories as pawing object, biting object, alerting posture, drinking, slapping the other bear, stretching, shaking the entire body or parts of the body.

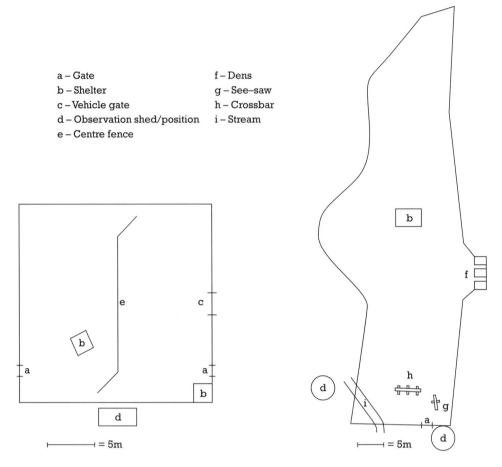

a – Gate   f – Dens
b – Shelter   g – See–saw
c – Vehicle gate   h – Crossbar
d – Observation shed/position   i – Stream
e – Centre fence

Figure 20.1 Plans of bear enclosures at Tremont (left) and Goldrush (right)
Source: Jordan and Burghardt (1986)

- Class O: Objects oriented towards or interacted with, such as grass, flowers (living matter), straw, leaves (non-living matter), mouse, dog, observer (animals), apples, nuts (water and food), stone, fence (other objects), body excretions, air and soil.

Procedure

All the bears were observed for about an hour each morning over a period of two-and-a-half years (=146 hours). At each time interval a unit of behaviour from each class was recorded. For Class F it was possible for two units to co-occur, in which case it was decided to record only the less usual behaviour. This decision was based on the principle that the information value of a behaviour was inversely proportional to its frequency of occurrence.

Two observers collected data independently and gained inter-observer agreement of between 80 and 98% in different sessions, averaging 88.6%.

Table 20.1 Class P behavioural descriptions

Activity Level 1: Reclining postures	Code
Dorsal lying with all four legs extended upwards	P6
Ventral lying with four legs extended forwards on both sides or with the front legs extended forwards but the rear legs both to one side	P7
Lateral lying with the front and rear legs all to one side	P8
Lying (or sitting, front legs supported) in a tree or other similarly elevated object	P28

Activity Level 2: Sitting and quadrupedal standing postures	
Standing quadrupedally	P3
Sitting erect or semi-erect with forelimbs elevated	P4
Sitting with forelimbs touching the ground	P5
Standing bipedally or quadrupedally in a tree or similarly elevated object	P29

Activity Level 3: Bipedal standing postures and slow locomotion	
Standing bipedally erect or semi-erect while touching an object with the forelimbs	P1
Standing bipedally erect or semi-erect with no support from the forelimbs	P2
Walking quadrupedally	P11
Walking stiffly, forelegs locked at the knee	P18
Rolling over	P33
Backing up	P34

Activity Level 4: Rapid or vigorous activity, including running, jumping and climbing	
Running	P19
Ascending (typically trees)	P24
Descending (typically trees)	P27
Running a short distance, then walking quickly	P32
Jumping (all legs off the ground simultaneously)	P35

RESULTS

Within-session effects

For each two-minute period a calculation was made of the activity level (AL) for each bear. Thus, for example, in the first two-minute period 42% of the total activity of Bear A was classed as AL1 (Activity Level 1 as defined in Table 20.1). By plotting all 30 two-minute periods it was possible to identify any increase or decrease in activity during a session. A scatter plot was made for each activity level. The closer the slope was to zero, the less reactivity (activity) was shown by the bear. Figures 20.2 and 20.3 show two different activity levels for two different bears.

When all the bears' activity levels were considered, it was possible to conclude that changes in rate of activity at Goldrush were minimal. This was not true at Tremont however, where both bears showed an increase in AL1 activities and a concomitant decrease in the others.

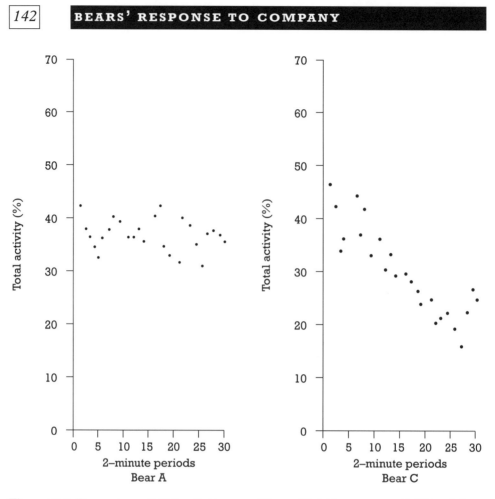

Figure 20.2 Percentage of AL1 activity for Bear A at Tremont. There is no significant increase in this activity level
Source: Jordan and Burghardt (1986)

Figure 20.3 Percentage of AL2 activity for Bear C at Goldrush. There is a noticeable decrease in this activity level
Source: Jordan and Burghardt (1986)

It is possible that the patterns of increase or decrease in behaviour were due to other consistent environmental changes, such as the height of the sun. The bears at Goldrush, however, were more directly exposed to the sun and yet showed least change.

Long-term habituation

A second means of assessing reactivity was in terms of alerting and attending behaviours: standing erect, looking, sniffing and pacing. Alerting was not a useful measure within sessions because it only occurred at the beginning of the session or when the observer made a sudden loud noise or moved quickly.

Over the long term, alerting and attending behaviours generally decreased (see Figure 20.4). This may have been a sign of long-term habituation, or of maturation.

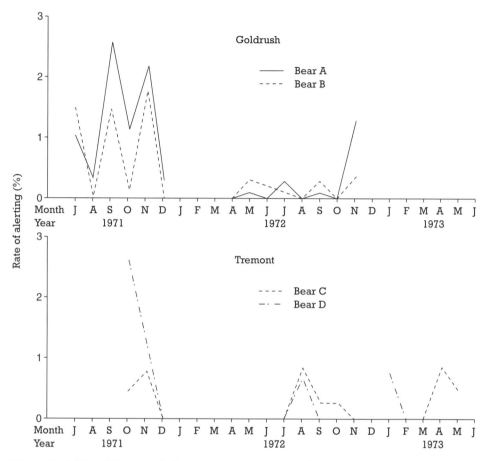

Figure 20.4 Monthly rate of alerting behaviours at Goldrush and Tremont. The fact that Goldrush was closed to the public from October to May may help to explain the data

Source: Jordan and Burghardt (1986)

DISCUSSION

Jordan and Burghardt concluded that their study demonstrated that black bears do respond to the presence of people with consistent and predictable behavioural changes.

The bears at Goldrush were less disturbed by the research observers than those at Tremont. This can be accounted for by various factors. First of all, the Goldrush enclosure was larger and enclosed by two concentric fences. At Tremont the bears were fed before each observation period by one of the observers, which may have heightened their awareness of the observers. Moreover, the bears may have been more aware of the observers because their enclosure was smaller and the observers closer.

More importantly, at Goldrush there was greater general activity – more visitors and more noises such as a railway train in the park. This meant that the bears habituated to all stimulation. The Tremont bears were not in a public park and were rarely visited. The irony of this is that more naturalistic observation was possible in the less naturalistic environment where the bears had the opportunity to habituate to outside influences.

The importance of this research for naturalistic observation in general is to underline the role of participant reactivity and the need for measures to control it. This may well be most important in the wild, where animals have less opportunity to habituate to human presence. Even where animals have habituated towards their observers, their behaviour may be affected. For example, Van Lawick-Goodall (1971) noted that the chimpanzees who had become accustomed to her presence would then approach her, which reduced her ability to observe them in their natural state.

It might be possible to use remote-sensing devices to eliminate reactivity, but this may be impractical.

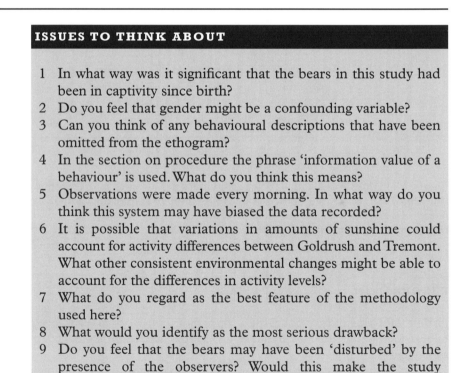

ISSUES TO THINK ABOUT

1 In what way was it significant that the bears in this study had been in captivity since birth?
2 Do you feel that gender might be a confounding variable?
3 Can you think of any behavioural descriptions that have been omitted from the ethogram?
4 In the section on procedure the phrase 'information value of a behaviour' is used. What do you think this means?
5 Observations were made every morning. In what way do you think this system may have biased the data recorded?
6 It is possible that variations in amounts of sunshine could account for activity differences between Goldrush and Tremont. What other consistent environmental changes might be able to account for the differences in activity levels?
7 What do you regard as the best feature of the methodology used here?
8 What would you identify as the most serious drawback?
9 Do you feel that the bears may have been 'disturbed' by the presence of the observers? Would this make the study unethical?

REFERENCES

Jordan, R. H. and Burghardt, G.M. (1986) Employing an ethogram to detect reactivity of black bears (*Ursus americanus*) to the presence of humans. *Ethology* (formerly Zeitschrift fur Tierpsychologie), *73(2)*, 89–115.

Van Lawick-Goodall, J. (1971) *In the shadow of man*. Boston: Houghton Mifflin.

RECOMMENDED READING

Haynes, S.N. and Horne, W.F. (1982) Reactivity in behavioural observation: A review. *Journal of Behavioural Assessment, 4*, 369–85.

OPTIMUM SEARCH STRATEGIES

Key terms: Participant reactivity, bears, naturalistic observation.

Do-it-yourself: A Suggested Design

Hypothesis   Bears are more active at the beginning of an observation session than at the end.
You might select a different animal and a different target behaviour, adapting your hypothesis accordingly.

Participants   Zoo animals.

Design   This is a naturalistic observation making use of an ethogram.

- Conduct a pilot study. This will enable you to decide on behavioural categories for an ethogram and also give you an opportunity to become familiar with, and resolve, any problems associated with conducting the observation.
- Finalise the ethogram. This includes deciding on a system of abbreviations or codes.
- Decide on the behaviour-sampling procedures, for example, how often to make your observations and for how long.
- You should consider observer bias and reliability, and you may decide to have more than one observer.
- Include other records of the observer, such as a plan of the enclosure and a description of the animals.

Ethical considerations
- You must discuss your project with the zoo administration and seek their informed consent.
- You must consider any effects your observations will have on the animals and on members of the public.

Controls
- Inter-observer agreement, if you are able to work with more than one observer.
- Systematic means of recording observations.
- Systematic means of sampling behaviour.
- Standardised conditions.

Materials
- Ethogram, paper and pencils.
- Stop-watch.
- Camera (optional).

Analysis
- Descriptive statistics: means, clearly labelled tables and graphs to illustrate frequencies of particular behaviours. You can use a scattergram to illustrate changes in activity level during the course of each session.
- Related test of difference. Work with data for one animal over many days and compare activity levels at the beginning and end of a session.
- Unrelated test of difference. Compare the behaviour of different animals.

WRITING THE REPORT

Your report should be readable, and it should be detailed but not over long. Most colleges, universities and exam boards expect a report of about 1,500 to 2,000 words, excluding tables and appendices. (You should check what is expected with your school or college.) It should use the same divisions as most journal articles, except in some cases of qualitative research.

ABSTRACT (SUMMARY)

About 150 words. This allows the reader to gather the essential details of the study: aims, methods, results and conclusions. This should be written last, as only then can it truly reflect the actual contents of the report.

INTRODUCTION

About 400 words. This section outlines previous research. It should not be a general essay but just provide the background for your predictions (hypotheses). A one-sentence statement of the general field is quite acceptable, then move on to specific research. The ability to be selective demonstrates your understanding. Don't include material which is more relevant to the discussion section, although you may later refer to points made in the introduction.

RESEARCH AIMS AND HYPOTHESIS

State your predictions formally and unambiguously. In journal articles this is written as the last part of the introduction.

The hypothesis should be given in the present tense and does not have to include the word 'significant'. For example, to write 'girls are more intelligent than boys' is as acceptable as 'girls are significantly more intelligent than boys'. Some people like to see the direction of the research hypothesis stated and also justified.

Journal articles do not include the null hypothesis, but it is often expected in a student report.

METHOD

About 400 words. You should provide precise details of what you did, so that another person can replicate your study. This section can be broken down into the following:

- *Participants*: Details of participants, including researchers. Sampling procedures.
- *Design*: The decisions you made before starting the actual study, such as the experimental groups, ethical considerations, controls, apparatus and materials (actual materials such as observation check lists, questionnaires and standardised instructions, should be placed in the appendices).
- *Procedures*: What you actually did.

RESULTS

Descriptive statistics include summary tables and graphs. Any raw data that you wish to include should be placed in an appendix, but a summary is quite sufficient.

Don't overdo the descriptive statistics, for example, drawing several different graphs of the same data. Choose the representation which gives the reader the clearest insight into the way your data are distributed. Make sure you carefully label graphs, including a clear title. You should always use graph paper.

Inferential statistics are used to indicate the significance of the findings. Select an appropriate test (see Appendix II). Any calculations should be placed in the appendices, and referred to in the main text. In this section of your report you should state the statistic calculated, its significance and whether you will accept or reject your hypothesis.

DISCUSSION

About 400 words. First, discuss the theoretical significance of your findings, with reference to your aims/hypotheses and the research outlined in the introduction.

Second, consider the limitations and modifications of your method, and the implications (applications) of your results. You might propose ideas for extensions of this study or further research.

REFERENCES

This is not a bibliography. You should list alphabetically all the journal articles and books to which you have referred, using the standard form employed in this book (see, for example, page 134).

APPENDICES

Include raw data, calculations and questionnaires or other stimulus materials. Do not include answers from each participant.

REPORT CHECKLIST

ABSTRACT

❑ Have you summarised what the study is about?

❑ Have you stated your predictions?

❑ Have you described the essentials of the method?

❑ Have you given some details about the participants and where the research was conducted?

❑ What did you discover? Give a statement of your results.

❑ What is the importance of your research? Suggest applications or further research possibilities.

INTRODUCTION

❑ Is the introduction concise and specific to the topic studied (not like an essay)?

❑ Have you described one or two relevant studies (but no more than three)?

❑ Does your introduction explain how you arrived at your research aims and hypothesis?

AIMS AND HYPOTHESES

❑ Why have you studied this topic? Have you stated your aims?

❑ Have you stated an unambiguous alternate and null hypothesis? (Not all students are required to include the latter.)

❑ Is the hypothesis stated in the present tense?

❑ Have you stated, and justified, the direction of your hypothesis?

METHOD

❑ Have you stated the research design?

❑ Have you explained why each design decision was made?

❏ For an experiment: Have you described the different conditions (if relevant)?

❏ For an observation: Have you described the methods you used, for example, a behavioural grid?

❏ Have you stated the independent variable (IV) and dependent variable (DV), or co-variables (for a correlational study)?

❏ Have you explained any controls you used? And why they were used?

❏ Have you mentioned ethical considerations?

❏ Have you mentioned all researchers involved?

❏ Have you described the participants and the population from which they were drawn?

❏ Have you stated how the participants were selected?

❏ Have you stated how the participants were allocated to conditions?

❏ Have you included all apparatus and materials you used (in the appendices)?

❏ Have you included answers to any tests or questionnaires (in the appendices)?

❏ Have you described the standardised procedure?

❏ Have you described or included standardised instructions given to participants (in the appendices)?

❏ Have you provided sufficient detail for someone else to replicate your study ?

RESULTS

❏ Have you given a summary table of the results, numbered and fully titled?

❏ Have you provided some graphical representation of the results?

❏ Have you labelled all axes on graphs, columns on data tables, and given clear titles?

❏ Have you justified your choice of any statistical tests used?

❏ Have you included the calculations in the appendix?

❏ Does your statement of conclusion include details on the level of significance, the critical and observed values, the degrees of freedom, and whether the hypothesis was one- or two-tailed?

❏ Have you stated the conclusion in terms of the original hypotheses?

DISCUSSION

❏ Have you stated what your results mean in relation to your hypothesis?

❏ Did you explain how you obtained such results?

❏ Have you compared your results to those of other studies?

❏ What was wrong (or right) with your design and methods?

❏ Are all criticisms presented with detailed explanation/justification?

❏ How would you improve the study if you were to do it again?

❏ Have you included any ideas for follow-up studies?

❏ Could your findings be applied to any real-life situation?

❏ Is the discussion concise (no longer than 500 words)?

REFERENCES

❏ Have you included all (and only) the references mentioned?

❏ Have you followed the correct form for presenting references?

APPENDICES

❏ Are these clearly labelled and well set out?

REPORT STYLE

❏ Have you checked your spelling?

❏ Is your project in a folder that can be easily opened?

❏ Is your project shorter than 2,000 words? If not, cut it.

A STUDENT REPORT

An experiment to investigate and compare two forms of memory recall, imagery and rehearsal

ABSTRACT

This study concerns memory. It investigates two different forms of recall (imagery and rehearsal). The experiment involved 24 undergraduates, an opportunity sample. All were aged between 18 and 26. A list of 20 word pairs was read out for the participants to memorise. Ten pairs were to be memorised using imagery, ten using rehearsal. At the end of the experiment, participants were given one word of a pair and asked to write down the other word.

A t-test was carried out on the results of the experiment. The observed value of t was 5.1. This showed the results of the experiment to be significant, demonstrating that more imagery word pairs were recalled than for rehearsal.

[*The title should give a good idea of what the study is about but should not be too long, as it is in this example.*

The abstract is 114 words long, which is good. It could include a few more details to help the reader better understand what was involved in the procedure. For example, what does 'memorised using imagery' mean? It could also state the hypothesis and include details about the level at which the hypothesis was accepted or rejected, plus the critical value of the statistic. It would also be useful to include a brief statement about what the results mean.

Does this summary give you a good picture of what is to follow?]

INTRODUCTION

The memory involves three main features: registration, storage and retrieval. Registration is how information to be stored is selected, storage concerns the ability to retrieve information and how we remember information.

[*Not very clear!*]

There are three forms of storage: sensory memory, short-term memory (STM) and long-term memory (LTM). Atkinson and Shiffrin (1968, 1971) showed the difference between STM and LTM in their multistore model.

The short-term memory can be broken down into three parts. First, capacity – the

STM is limited to six or seven bits. Second, duration – information can be held in the STM for 15 to 30 seconds though this can be extended through rehearsal and repetition. Third, coding concerns how information can be processed, stored and represented by the memory system. This is usually acoustically (through rehearsal) in the STM although it can be visual, but this takes more time.

The LTM's capacity is unlimited although not all the things stored can be recalled. The duration is from a few minutes to one's whole lifetime. There are at least two forms of coding: semantic code which concerns verbal meaning, and imagery/visual code which concerns images and pictures.

There are a number of forms of retrieval that can be used. One of which is imagery, for example, to remember visual information we can associate it with some kind of visual image.

Pavio (1969) developed a dual coding model. He suggested that two coding systems are used to represent information in memory. These are verbal/linguistic and verbal/imaginal. These two coding systems are joined together so it is possible for an image to come from a verbal label and a verbal label to come from an image as opposed to just using one code to recall information.

Begg and Pavio (1969) carried out a number of experiments which manipulated the main variable through the classification of words into 'concrete' and 'abstract'. 'Concreteness' concerned how easily a word brought up a mental image.

The results showed that imagery connections were made faster for concrete than abstract words. Also, more concrete than abstract words were recalled. This indicates that, because we have images of concrete objects already stored in the LTM, it is easier to retrieve these kinds of words because participants can use information from two coded forms (imaginal and verbal).

An experiment by Sachs (1967) gave evidence of the dual code theory. It showed that when participants were asked to remember sentences they sometimes found it hard to remember wording but were unlikely to forget the meaning of the sentence. Participants were also less likely to notice a sentence had changed wording as much as they noticed a change in meaning. This is because participants formed a picture of the meaning.

[*This introduction is too long. It is already 450 words. What parts would you leave out?*
Good points: Respectable attempt to report empirical research in student's own words, indicating an effort to grasp the meaning.
Bad points: The beginning is not highly relevant and detracts from the selectivity of the literature review.]

Bower (1972) found that if participants formed mental images of pairs of unrelated nouns (for example, dog and bicycle) and made the two interact together (a dog riding a bicycle), recall was better than when participants simply memorised the words. The more bizarre the image the better.

However, there is also evidence to refute Pavio's ideas. Pylyshyn (1973) argued that if you consider the amount of storage we would need to hold detailed copies of everything we see, it does not seem realistic. Also would the images in our LTMs be how we see the outside world?

There would also be problems concerning retrieval being inefficient because it would involve re-perceiving and analysing all the images to 'see' what was there before the images could be used. Another problem concerns retrieving the right picture through a word. A single word can correspond to many pictures.

Pylyshyn offered the alternative view that we form pictures in our memory of general descriptions, they exist as 'analysed entities'. He believes we can reconstruct pictures from abstract or general descriptions which we have already stored. This makes us believe we have pictures stored.

AIM

The aim of the experiment is to discover whether the use of imagery as a form of recall produces higher results than the use of rehearsal.

EXPERIMENTAL HYPOTHESIS

The results of the memory recall experiment will show that the number of word pairs recalled for imagery will be significantly higher than for rehearsal.

NULL HYPOTHESIS

The results of the memory recall experiment will show no significant difference between the number of word pairs recalled for imagery compared to rehearsal.

[*The latter paragraphs of the introduction really belong in the discussion. It doesn't make sense to go ahead and test Pavio's theory when you have just suggested it may be wrong. The hypothesis does not develop logically from the discussion. The student has written the hypothesis in the future, which is not desirable.*
Entire section is 720 words long.]

METHOD

This experiment involved two different conditions of recall: imagery and rehearsal. The experiment took place on a Tuesday afternoon. The participants were from a sample of 24 undergraduates who were available at the time. The sample comprised 18 females and 6 males between the ages of 18 and 26 years old.

[*It might have helped to use subheadings to break up the method section, such as conditions, participants, procedure, controls, ethical considerations.*]

The experiment involved the researcher reading out a list of 20 word pairs with an approximate 10-second gap between each pair. The participants had to learn each pair using one of two techniques: rehearsal (repeating word pairs four times) or imagery (forming a mental image with two words interacting together). There were 10 rehearsal pairs and 10 imagery pairs. Before the word pair was read out the participants were told whether it was to be remembered through rehearsal or imagery. When all the word pairs had been read out the participants counted backwards from 99 in threes until told to stop. They were then told the first word in each word pair and were asked to write down its partner.

The design used was repeated measures. All 24 participants took part in remembering both rehearsal and imagery word pairs under the same conditions.

The independent variable was the two different conditions: imagery and rehearsal. The dependent variable was the number of word pairs recalled.

Order effects were minimised by controlling the time of day the experiment took place, the location and the fact that standardised instructions were read to all participants. Order effects were also counterbalanced by changing the order of presentation so that half of the participants carried out the rehearsal condition first and imagery second, while the other half of the participants reversed this order. The test words were also counterbalanced.

Obviously not everything can be controlled. Some people might have used imagery techniques without consciously deciding to do so while they should have been using rehearsal. In addition, the feelings of individuals on the day of the experiment cannot be controlled. Some participants might have been more tired than others. Some might have had a full day of lectures whereas others might have been relaxing all day. These factors may affect the results.

[This paragraph belongs in the discussion. How might the problem be overcome?
Could you replicate this experiment? The word lists were given in an appendix though there is no reference to this in this section. There is no explanation of how word pairs were assigned to conditions, nor of how the word pairs were selected.
What about the standardised instructions? Did participants know what the experiment was about? Were they debriefed?
The order of this material is annoying, because we are told what was done before we know how it was designed (procedure before design).
The section is probably too short, only 350 words.]

RESULTS

The results of the experiment clearly show that more words were recalled by more people for imagery than rehearsal (see Appendix 1).

[It would have been helpful to see a summary table of this data in the text, such as the means for each set of data. The graphs could be presented here rather than in the appendix as they give you a feel for the data.]

A t-test was used to analyse the results and a significant result was found. For $N=24$, the critical value of $t=1.714$ ($p<0.05$ one-tailed test). As the observed value$=5.1$, we can reject the null hypothesis and conclude that imagery as a form of recalling word pairs is superior to rehearsal (see Appendix 3).

[You might compare the way the student has reported significance here with the style used in journal articles (see, for example, the results sections throughout the book).]

DISCUSSION

The results of the experiment show that in general, participants were able to recall higher numbers of imagery word pairs than rehearsal word pairs (Appendix 1 shows this).

After running a *t*-test on the results this confirmed the results to be valid (see Appendix 3). The critical value was 1.714 and the observed *t*-value was found to be higher than this (5.1). This shows the results to be significant.

[This specific material is not appropriate in the discussion. What is needed is a statement of the results in 'plain English'; for example, 'The results support the view that the use of imagery enhances recall as compared with rehearsal'.]

These results would appear to support Pavio's dual code theory because when participants use imagery as a form of recall, they are also using a form of verbal coding because the words are spoken to them (verbal) and they then transform them into images. So they are using two forms of coding and therefore are able to recall more word pairs than when they just use one form.

Most of the words used for the experiment were 'concrete' words (see Appendix 2). We already have quite strong images of these things. This may have affected the results in some way.

Bower and Winzenz (1970) might argue that people encode meaningful relationships between the word pairs (for example, heart and water) and so this could be another factor that would aid recall other than rehearsal or imagery.

One of the limits of the experiment is that when looking at the results there are a few answers that go against the hypothesis and general findings. For example, participant number 1 had a score of 7 for imagery and 9 for rehearsal. The few people who did score highly for rehearsal (6 or above) seemed to be the Japanese students. This raises questions as to why. Could it be because of the different language? Or maybe differences in the way they have been taught previously? A possible way to find out would be to conduct the experiment in the participant's first language and to see if the pattern reoccurs. The study could be extended to different cultures or compared between the two genders.

[There is a tendency for students to introduce the possibility of a gender difference without any real foundation. The other points made in this discussion are good, although some could be elaborated to demonstrate understanding.]

Another limitation to the results would be the fact that a number of students said they sometimes found it hard not to form mental images when they were supposed to be repeating the words only. This could be solved by having the first 10 words as rehearsal and the last 10 as images, or two independent groups could be used, one tested just on imagery and the other on rehearsal.

The implications of the results show that the memory can be greatly improved through the use of imagery. This could be applied to many tasks in life. It could be used in learning languages or when needing to remember a shopping list. It could even be applied when revising for an exam.

[*This discussion is only 450 words long, which is adequate but compared to the rest of the report perhaps a little on the short side. All the main things have been included: reference to other research, critical appraisal of method, further research ideas and real-life applications.*]

REFERENCES

Atkinson, R., Smith, E., Bem, D.B. and Hilgard, E. (1990) *Introduction to psychology*. London: HBJ.
Coolican, H. (1994) *Research methods and statistics in psychology*, 2nd edn. London: Hodder & Stoughton.
Open University (1981) Imagery and memory, from DS 202 *Summer School Project Booklet*.

[*This is a bibliography, not a list of references. The actual references are missing, for example,* Pavio, A. (1969) Mental imagery in associative learning and memory. *Psychological Review, 76, 241–63.*

Every reference cited in the text should be given in full here, in the reference section.]

APPENDIX 1

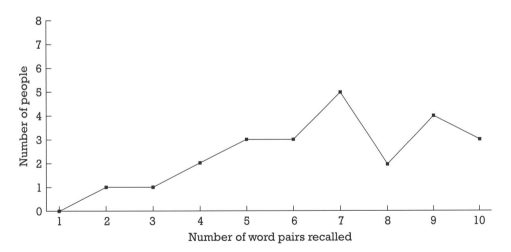

Figure 1 Number of word pairs recalled in imagery condition

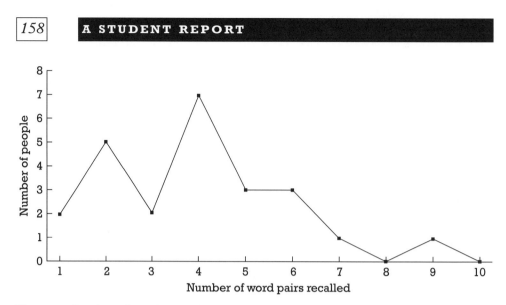

Figure 2 Number of word pairs recalled in rehearsal condition

APPENDIX 2

The list of techniques and word pairs used in an experiment to investigate imagery and rehearsal as methods of recall.

TECHNIQUE	WORD PAIRS
Repeat	Rabbit – House
Repeat	Boy – Rope
Image	Shoe – Mountain
Repeat	Table – Skull
Image	Doctor – Flag
Image	Book – Fish
Repeat	Slave – Party
Image	Lamp – Bird
Image	Heart – Water
Repeat	Ladder – Baby
Repeat	Teacher – Pudding
Image	Mule – Dress
Repeat	Kettle – Fox
Image	Snake – Fire
Image	Tree – Queen
Repeat	Flower – Money
Image	Harp – Elephant
Repeat	Bear – Candle
Repeat	Clock – Moon
Image	Horse – Potato

APPENDIX 3

Table to show results of the *t*-test

n	*df*	*t*	*Critical value*	*p*
24	23	5.1	1.714	<0.05

[*Some further details of the data should be included here, such as a summary of the raw data, some of the* t *calculations, and a comment on whether the hypothesis should be accepted or rejected.*]

APPENDIX I: USEFUL WORDS

WORD FREQUENCIES FROM THE THORNDIKE–LORGE WORD LIST

The numbers given show the frequency of each word per million.

3	algebra, daffodil, deduction, distraction, galaxy, greed, heredity, hindrance, hostage, immunity, inducement, insolence, keg, labyrinth, locker, mileage, molecule, outsider, pollution, retailer, scorpion, shotgun, stagecoach, sunburn, supplication, truce
4	avalanche, cleanness, courtship, dreamer, ensemble, exclusion, fantasy, festivity, flask, freedom, honeycomb, hypothesis, impact, ingratitude, irony, mastery, pact, passageway, performer, recital, ritual, suppression, vocation
5	adversity, bandit, equity, gaiety, gilt, graduation, heroism, multiplication, nightfall, piston, poster, profile, stub, underworld, vacuum, venom, vigilance
6	alligator, belongings, blister, chasm, leopard, mammal, pelt, phantom, photograph
7	abduction, anecdote, appliance, athletics, caravan, core, episode, epistle, exertion, firmament, garret, goblet, gore, hurricane, leaflet, lemonade, lobster, magnetite, opium, perception, periodical, prestige, rheumatism, satire
8	ambulance, bacteria, basement, bouquet, bungalow, crag, creator, deceit, demon, essence, glacier, infection, instructor, mathematics, mosquito, outcome, reptile, spinach, utensil, velocity, violation, whale
9	bravery, chaos, combustion, corpse, daybreak, discretion, edifice, exhaustion, friction, microscope, nun, ownership, revolver, robbery

continued

10	illusion, malice, orchestra, promotion
11	refrigerator, sadness, spire
12	hostility, madness, proprietor, saloon
13	hearing, nymph, skull, umbrella, vehicle
14	brute, gravity, sultan, tempest, volcano
15	alcohol, obedience
16	abode, cigar
17	comedy, jealousy, pudding, reminder, trumpet
18	musician
19	amazement, blacksmith, bronze, builder, cane, caterpillar, contribution, crisis, decoration, determination, dove, edition, emergency, fatigue, fireplace, formation, hardship, jelly, landscape, loyalty, market, nonsense, nursery, panic, portrait, session, socialist, strawberry, tank, thicket, vigour
20	admiral, array, charter, co-operation, decree, democracy, errand, fowl, harp, hatred, hillside, ink, macaroni, mischief, monarch, monk, plank, quest, settler, sensation, singer, slipper, toast, vanity
21	ambassador, ankle, captive, circuit, code, cradle, devotion, dirt, discipline, economy, enterprise, fabric, foam, institute, menace, moisture, reaction, sulphur, vest
22	anxiety, assault, attribute, bullet, butcher, butterfly, disposition, goddess, gratitude, ignorance, infant, jail, lark, moss, nephew, permission, reflection, research, revolt, spray, tomb, tribute
23	banner, boss, claw, disaster, drama, facility, headquarters, hound, oats, investigation, legislation, restaurant, sovereign, truck, warmth
24	agony, engagement, gem, injury, intimate, link, miracle, poverty, sunset, tablespoon, thorn
25	background, ceremony, comparison, costume, daylight, fox, frog, oxygen, painter, sickness, speaker, welfare
26	attendant, comrade, conquest, distinction, elbow, fisherman, geese, golf, hoof, impulse, interview, item, jury, mast, misery, piano, pole

continued

27	banker, baron, intellect, kettle, lemon, lime, maker, mantle, mood, odour, patent, pepper, procession, robber, sauce, scarlet, tendency, tragedy, vapour
28	competition, examination, gallery, lecture, profession, rattle, salad, snake, stain, steamer, thief
29	beggar, blessing, breeze, folly, harness, hint, incident, mule, peach, prosperity, sentiment, substitute, swamp, twilight, unit
30	angle, cord, genius, inhabitant
31	agreement, explanation, fork
32	candidate, cellar, ghost, joke

Source: Thorndike, E.L. and Lorge, I. (1944) *The teacher's wordbook of 30,000 words*. New York: Teacher's College, Bureau of Publications.

WORDS FOR POLAR OPPOSITES

A check list of polar opposites used by Asch (1946) in his experiments on impression formation.

generous	ungenerous		humane	ruthless
wise	shrewd		good-looking	unattractive
happy	unhappy		persistent	unstable
good-natured	irritable		serious	frivolous
humorous	humourless		restrained	talkative
sociable	unsociable		altruistic	self-centred
popular	unpopular		imaginative	hard-headed
reliable	unreliable		strong	weak
important	unimportant		honest	dishonest

Source: Asch, S. (1946) Forming impressions of personality. *Journal of Abnormal and Social Psychology*, *41*, 258–90.

WORDS HIGH AND LOW IN LIKABLENESS AND MEANINGFULNESS

Anderson (1968) asked 100 participants to rate 555 words for attractiveness on a scale of 0–6 and a scale of 0–4 for meaningfulness (0 = 'I have almost no idea of the meaning of this word', 4 = 'I have a very clear and definite understanding of this word'). The top score after adding together both dimensions was 573 for *sincere*, and the bottom score was 26 for *liar*.

TOP 20 for likableness and meaning		BOTTOM 20 for likableness and meaning	
sincere	reliable	ill-mannered	unkind
honest	warm	unfriendly	untrustworthy
understanding	kind	hostile	malicious
loyal	friendly	loud-mouthed	obnoxious
truthful	happy	selfish	untruthful
trustworthy	unselfish	narrow-minded	dishonest
intelligent	humorous	rude	cruel
dependable	responsible	conceited	mean
thoughtful	cheerful	greedy	phoney
considerate	trustful	insincere	liar

Source: Anderson, N.H. (1968) Likableness ratings of 555 personality-trait words. *Journal of Personality and Social Psychology, 9(3)*, 272–9. Copyright © 1968 by the American Psychological Association. Reprinted with permission.

WORDS OF HIGH AND LOW FREQUENCY OF USAGE

Postman, Bruner and McGinnies (1948, *Journal of Abnormal Psychology*) found that words representing more valued interests were recognised more quickly (lower duration threshold) than less valued words. In addition, frequency of word usage is inversely related to the visual duration threshold. Solomon and Howes (1951) repeated this study, but controlled for word frequency of occurrence using the Thorndike–Lorge word counts.

Categories	theoretical	economic	political	aesthetic	religious	social
frequent (valued)	scientific	automobile	liberties	poetry	churches	hospitality
	physics	market	lawyer	picture	heavenly	friendly
	intellectual	savings	debating	painter	spiritual	service
	knowledge	economics	initiative	orchestra	reverence	charitable
	education	earthly	government	literary	religious	sympathy
infrequent	inductive	limousine	uncoerced	elegies	chancels	conviviality
	statics	broker	barrister	vignette	celestial	amicable
	percipience	frugality	rebuttal	etcher	psychical	benign
	erudition	assets	assiduous	ensemble	beatific	altruistic
	pedagogue	mundane	judiciary	metaphor	theistic	condolence

Source: Solomon, R.L. and Howes, D.H. (1951) Word frequency, personal values, and visual duration thresholds. *Psychological Review, 58*, 256–70.

CATTELL'S 16 PERSONALITY FACTORS

The following pairs of personality opposites are used in Cattell's personality test.

A	reserved	warm-hearted
B	concrete thinker	abstract thinker
C	affected by feelings	emotionally stable
E	submissive	assertive
F	sober	happy-go-lucky
G	expedient	conscientious
H	shy	venturesome
I	tough-minded	tender-minded
L	trusting	suspicious
M	practical	imaginative
N	forthright	shrewd
O	self-assured	apprehensive
Q_1	conservative	experimenting
Q_2	group-dependent	self-sufficient
Q_3	undisciplined self-conflict	controlled
Q_4	relaxed	tense

Detailed description of pairs:

A	cool, detached, aloof	A	easygoing, participating, outgoing
B	practically minded	B	intellectual interests
C	emotionally less stable, easily upset	C	faces reality, calm, mature
E	mild, accommodating	E	dominant, aggressive, competitive
F	prudent, serious, taciturn	F	impulsively lively, enthusiastic
G	disregards rules, feels few obligations	G	persevering, oralistic, strait-laced
H	restrained, timid, threat-sensitive	H	socially bold, uninhibited, spontaneous
I	self-reliant, realistic, no-nonsense	I	gentle, overprotective, sensitive
L	adaptable, free of jealousy, easy to get along with	L	self-opinionated, hard to fool
M	careful, conventional, regulated by practical matters, bohemian	M	wrapped up in inner urgencies, careless of external realities
N	natural, artless, unpretentious	N	calculating, worldly, penetrating
O	confident, complacent	O	self-reproaching, worrying, troubled
Q1	respecting established ideas, tolerant of traditional difficulties	Q1	liberal, analytical, free-thinking
Q2	a 'joiner', a good follower	Q2	prefers own decisions, resourceful
Q3	follows own urges, careless of rules	Q3	socially precise, compulsive, social
Q4	tranquil, composed	Q4	frustrated, driven, overwrought

APPENDIX II: STATISTICAL TECHNIQUES

A statistic is:

- A number or numbers used to represent facts or data.
- The collection, classification and analysis of data.
- Procedures or formulas to enable a researcher to draw conclusions.

There are two categories:

- Descriptive statistics: numerical (for example, mean, mode, range, standard deviation), distributions (for example, normal) and graphical (for example, bar chart, scattergram) which are all ways of *describing* your data.
- Inferential statistics allow us to *test* our hypotheses. They are based on the mathematics of probability theory in order to make generalisations or draw inferences from sample data to the population.

Inferential statistics can be subdivided into:

- Parametric or non-parametric statistics.
- Tests of difference or correlation.

PARAMETRIC OR NOT

Non-parametric tests have fewer assumptions and have fewer requirements for their data. Parametric tests are more powerful (i.e. able to detect relationships) and require that the data are:

- At interval or ratio level.
- Similar variance (determined using an F-test).
- Drawn from a normally distributed population.

You can use a non-parametric test on any data but they are less effective at detecting differences. However, most parametric tests are said to be robust and their validity is not affected by even quite marked departures from the criteria.

TWO SAMPLE TESTS OF DIFFERENCE

When you have two samples of data, you need to know whether one is significantly different from the other. For parametric statistics this is done by comparing the means and variances, whereas for non-parametric statistics the ranks of the differences are compared.

There are two questions:

- Are the samples related?
- Is the data parametric?

DATA	SAMPLE		PARAMETRIC
LEVEL	RELATED	UNRELATED	?
nominal	sign test (x)	Chi-squared (χ^2)	no
ordinal	Wilcoxon (T)	Mann–Whitney (U)	no
interval	related t-test (t)	independent t-test (t)	yes

DIFFERENCE TESTS WITH TWO OR MORE SAMPLES: ANOVA

ANOVA (analysis of variance) tests enable you to compare two or more sets of data, and to identify the source of variability. For example, two groups are both given treatments A and B. Variability can come from:

- The participants (i.e. participant variability within groups, which we want to minimise).
- The conditions (i.e. variability of scores due to the conditions, which is what we want to find).
- An interaction of participants with conditions (an *interaction* effect).
- Unexplained variability (the *error*).

	SAMPLE		
	RELATED	UNRELATED	MIXED (related and unrelated)
Non-parametric	Friedman (Trend: Page Trend Test)	Kruskal–Wallis (Trend: Jonkheere Trend Test)	
Parametric	One-way repeat measure ANOVA	One-way unrelated measure ANOVA	
Parametric (more than one IV)	Two-way or multi-factor repeat measure ANOVA	Two-way or multi-factor randomised/ unrelated ANOVA	Mixed factor ANOVA

One way ANOVA: Manipulation of one IV, at two or more levels (for one level use *t*-test).

Two-way or multi-factor ANOVA: more than one IV. Each IV is a *factor*. Each condition of the factor is a *level*. [NB: *The DV must be a continuous variable.*]

The result is an *F* ratio[1] (given with degrees of freedom) which can be given for:

- *Simple effects*: found on *t*-tests or one-way ANOVA.
- *Main effects*: when one IV has a consistent overall significant effect.
- *Interaction effects*: only found when using multi-factor ANOVA. No IV has an overall effect but the interaction of one factor with another factor produces a significant effect.

An example of this would be looking at the effect of age (IV) on driving ability (DV), by recording age group and experience (therefore no 'simple effects'). Possible results might be:

- *Main effect*: age affects driving ability.
- *Interaction effect*: age interacts with experience (Age × Experience), which in turn affects driving ability.

To analyse the data you calculate an *F* ratio and report in the following manner: $F(x_1, y) = $ and $F(x_2, y) = $, where

x_1 = degrees of freedom for the first IV (age)
x_2 = degrees of freedom for the second IV (experience)
y = degrees of freedom for the error term.

TESTS OF CORRELATION

Correlation can be tested using:

- Pearson's test (*r*) for parametric data.
- Spearman's *rho* for non-parametric data.
- Chi-squared (χ^2) is used when data is given, or can be grouped in frequencies.

ONE SAMPLE TESTS

- *One sample* t-*test* (*t*): compares the *mean* of a sample with the mean of a known or theoretical population.
- *One sample proportions test* (*z*): compares the *proportion* of cases in a sample with those in a known or theoretical population.
- *Chi-squared goodness of fit test (1 × N)*: tests whether a distribution is uniform, or according to a theoretically predicted distribution.

---

1 This *F* ratio or test is the same one we encountered earlier when testing to see if the variances of two samples were similar (to meet parametric criteria). In the ANOVA test, the *F* ratio is again a comparison of variance measures, but in this case it is the treatment variation divided by the error variation.

RECOMMENDED BOOKS ON RESEARCH DESIGN AND STATISTICS

Banister, P., Burman, E., Parker, I., Taylor, M. and Tindall, C. (1994) *Qualitative Methods in Psychology*. Buckingham: Open University Press. [A good discussion of qualitative methods and how to do them.]

Clegg, F. (1990) Simple statistics: A course book for the social sciences. Cambridge: Cambridge University Press. [User-friendly, with cartoons, book of main statistical methods.]

Coolican, H. (1994) *Research methods and statistics in psychology* (2nd edn). London: Hodder & Stoughton. [As the book below but more advanced – includes ANOVA.]

Coolican, H. (1996) *Introduction to research methods and statistics in Psychology* (2nd edn). London: Hodder & Stoughton. [A very clearly written book with exercises.]

Foster, J.J. and Parker, I. (1995) *Carrying out investigations in psychology*. Leicester: BPS Books. [Thorough descriptions of methods, report writing and statistics.]

Greene, J. and D'Oliveria, M. (1982) *Learning to use statistical tests in psychology: A student's guide*. Milton Keynes: Open University Press. [Very clear and user-friendly.]

Harris, P. (1986) *Designing and reporting experiments*. Milton Keynes: Open University Press [Brief details of all main issues, with SAQ.]

McIlveen, R., Higgins, L. and Wadeley, A. (1992) *BPS manual of psychology practicals*. Leicester: BPS Books. [Well-tested practicals with sections on each kind of method.]

Robson, C. (1993) *Real world research*. Oxford: Blackwell. [Similar to Foster and Parker but longer and with more specific examples of, for instance, questionnaire design.]